T0208528

The TRUTH for
FREEDOM
from
RELIGIOUS
BONDAGE,
SPIRITUAL SLAVERY
AND DESTRUCTION
of
CLIMATE CHANGE

The TRUTH for FREEDOM from RELIGIOUS BONDAGE, SPIRITUAL SLAVERY AND DESTRUCTION of CLIMATE CHANGE

Professor Donald E. Mbosowo. Ph.D.

THE TRUTH FOR FREEDOM FROM RELIGIOUS BONDAGE, SPIRITUAL SLAVERY AND DESTRUCTION OF CLIMATE CHANGE

Unless otherwise indicated, all scripture quotations are from The Holy Bible, English Standard Version® (ESV®). Copyright ©2001 by Crossway Bibles, a division of Good News Publishers. Used by permission. All rights reserved.

Scripture quotations marked NKJV are taken from the New King James Version. Copyright © 1982 by Thomas Nelson, Inc. Used by permission. All rights reserved.

Scripture quotations marked NIV are taken from the Holy Bible, New International Version®. NIV®. Copyright © 1973, 1978, 1984 by International Bible Society. Used by permission of Zondervan. All rights reserved. [Biblica]

Scripture quotations marked KJV are from the Holy Bible, King James Version (Authorized Version). First published in 1611. Quoted from the KJV Classic Reference Bible, Copyright © 1983 by The Zondervan Corporation.

iUniverse books may be ordered through booksellers or by contacting:

iUniverse
1663 Liberty Drive
Bloomington, IN 47403
www.iuniverse.com
1-800-Authors (1-800-288-4677)

Because of the dynamic nature of the Internet, any web addresses or links contained in this book may have changed since publication and may no longer be valid. The views expressed in this work are solely those of the author and do not necessarily reflect the views of the publisher, and the publisher hereby disclaims any responsibility for them.

Any people depicted in stock imagery provided by Getty Images are models, and such images are being used for illustrative purposes only.
Certain stock imagery © Getty Images.

ISBN: 978-1-5320-9117-9 (sc)
ISBN: 978-1-5320-9118-6 (e)

Print information available on the last page.

iUniverse rev. date: 12/11/2019

CONTENTS

ABOUT THE AUTHOR

Professor Donald E Mbosowo holds a B.A., M. A. and a Ph D. in sociology.

He is the founder and president of the Vineyard Ministries International Inc.,

He had the calling of the I AM upon his life in 1989. he had a vision of Jesus, the I AM in 1993, and was less interested in the call, but he finally accepted it when he had a divine encounter with the I AM in 1999 in a hotel in Tulsa, Oklahoma, United States.

He also served as an Elder in the Over-Comers Faith Center of the Church of God mission in Nigeria.

He also served as minister in the New Wine Church, and as an assistant minister in the Greater Restoration Temple in Mississippi.

The Greater Restoration Temple ordained him a minister on January 7th 2000, and he founded Vineyard Ministries International Inc.,

He taught at the University for twenty nine years and he is now paying attention to his calling in order to unfold and complete the interrupted mission given to Moses by the I AM and to present Jesus as the revealed I A M and as an African, who came to mediate, redeem and save humanity from the sufferings that resulted from the wars and fights between Lucifer-Satan-god and Eve-Devil- Goddess.

DEDICATION

I dedicate this book to those who have the spiritual awareness to speak the truth without fear, and to the entire African Race that will see the light and come out of the religious slavery.

CHAPTER ONE

Inspirational Note

I am putting up this note as an inspiration, whether you believe this or not, I advise you to listen to this truth. This planet earth is the current planet inhabited by a certain type of being called human. In this planet, we have many elements like water, trees, rocks, land, sand, oxygen etc. scientists have searched and found similar elements like water, rock, sand, oxygen in other previous planets, such as we have here on earth. All the similarities show that there were previous planets before planet earth.

The question is, what type of beings lived in those planets, and why were they either closed down or destroyed? I want everyone to pay attention. Those planets were inhabited by certain beings. Those planets were either closed down or destroyed because those beings worshipped the wrong creator and practiced religious and spiritual lies. The same thing will happen to this planet earth if we do not change, and follow the right creator and teach the truth, instead of worshipping the God and the Goddess of this world.

Revelation: I had a ministration in 1996, when I was a professor at Mississippi Valley State University. In the summer of 1996, I went for a walk in the morning at the Greenwood Park. As I was walking, a voice spoke to me that by the year 4000, there will be only 5 percent male population in the world, and all will eventually died out, and beings from another planet will come down and have sexual intercourse with women and a different type of beings will be produced to inhabit the earth. I was really concerned about it.

When I got home, I prayed and asked a question, whether it referred to only African men, and I had no answer. This means that the entire population of men in the world will be eradicated. I don't know why it will happen to the males. It may be because Adam listened to Eve, his partner in creation, and indirectly surrendered his authority to her to fulfill the promise that Lucifer, the tempter promise that she would not die, rather she will become like God, knowing good and evil (Gen. 3:5). That was when Eve achieved the status of goddess and has ruled the world for millions of years as discussed in detail in later chapters.

I have a sign in the western world where men go on their knees to propose to women for marriage. This is the reign of matrilineal system.

I have told a few people, but the reaction had been, if it is not in the Bible. I will not believe that God will allow all men to be eradicated. I stopped discussing my revelations with people until now that I decided to put some in this book. Another shocking revelation came in MARCH 2018. ON THE 20TH OF march 2018, at 5pm, I was thinking about the problems in this world, and I made a statement: 'when I die, I will go to hell and not heaven, because It looks like there is action in hell, and heaven may be boring'. Brothers and sisters, please listen, after one hour, so at 6pm, I had premonition of death and it was very strong. I went to my prayer altar and said that I did not want to die today. I prayed until 8pm and begged Jesus to spare my life. I was camped down. I went to bed at 9pm. In my sleep, I had a dream.

I was sitting in the living room in my house, and members of my family sat around me. I told them that if I die, nobody should dismantle any of my belongings. As soon as I said that, I found myself at the Edmond Cemetery with all members of my family. I told them to go home and not to touch any of my things in the house because I will be back in three days.

They left and two men – an Asian and a Caucasian appeared and came to me and they took me to a valley between two big buildings. Between the two buildings, was a big tunnel. They asked me to go into the tunnel. I went into the tunnel and arrived at a community. In the community, I saw only white women, who were sitting on the ground with their legs tugged in and their heads bent down. I looked at them and turned back into the tunel and arrived back at where I met the two men, but those men were not there anymore. I woke up.'

I waited on the Lord for three days without telling anyone in my family. After three days, I told a friend, and never told anyone until now that it appears in my book as a warning to the world for a change, because of the meaning of this dream as stated below.

When I prayed about this dream, the Holy Spirit told me the following:

1- I was given an experience to know what hell is because of my heartbroken about the sufferings of humanity.

2- You were transformed for the work you are called to do

3- The tunnel you entered is the female sex organ "vagina" that was created in the woman –Eve by Lucifer during the deception, and that tunnel must be closed, so that sexual intercourse between man and woman with sperm-pregnancy to produce evil being can come to an end. A man is sowing into the polluted system through the tunnel called "VAGINA", and the products are evil beings, because it has violated the divine spiritual sowing by the "Word" to become beings.

4- The reason I saw only Caucasian women in hell, is that the concept of hell was created by religious leaders to punish women because it was a woman who yielded to fallen angel Lucifer, and that brought problems to humanity. It is also for the women who will not be able to get back into the 'MAN" to become one as it was at first creation. There is no marriage in Heaven, and every women must go back into a man to become one as angel. The reason African women were not there in hell, is that Africans do not have a religion and did not join in the creation of religious concept of hell for women.

5- African women have been prevented from the religious hell, but Eve-Goddess in the world of witchcraft controls them. First the 'Man-Adam-Male' in African lineage was weakened, when he yielded to Eve's advise, and it is the duty of African men to rise and restore the male-Adam status that Jesus brought as the second Adam (Rom 5:19; 1 Cor 15:45); and this will create the spiritual road for African women to come back into the men to become one for the heavenly realm. This is very important because the position of Adam was weakened and made it difficult for women to go into the men and that led to the African witches now ruling the world of witchcraft and try to punish men who do not help.

6- When the two become one, the end will come, the woman came out of Adam=Man and must return to the man to restore the status of an angel since Heaven does not accommodate the two separate beings of male and female. This was disrupted by Lucifer, who messed up the divine partnership between Adam and Eve, and the established 'marriage' that the church does not know to direct people. This means that those women who will not be able to get back into where they came from, will end up in hell. It is the duty of a woman to preserve, love and nurture the man she will return to at the last days after life. The devil has deceived women and allowed them to rebel against their husbands. All these lead to disconnect from the men they married. Some women marry two, three times with different men, and have not planted the 'Soul-Tie' and 'Spiritual requirement' to secure men, they will go back into for the final preparation for Heaven. For your information, connection by the Spirit is for Jesus, the I AM for the Kingdom of Heaven of the I AM, the Creator, while connection by the soul is for Lucifer-God for the kingdom of God on earth's supernatural.

The major problem for women is that most women have not been able to secure the ELO space in men to go back to become one. The hidden secret is that the word 'love' is a shield and the 'Spirit' of love is 'affection' and affection is the power and energy that is projected out a wife into 'a husband' and that affection will touch the man and create the ELO in the man she will return into. This took place after Adam and Eve sinned and lost the divine partnership for procreation, and Lucifer established 'Marriage' between Adam and Eve and created his kind of love through sexual union.

Any wife who has affection for another man when she commits adultery, will not create a space for her to return because it is against the legal status and requirement for matrimony. The Holy Spirit told me that Sarah in the Bible was a beautiful woman and did not have affection for Abram, because she was of the same father with Abram and different mothers (gen 20:12) and marrying a sister as practiced by the Jews, might not have been practiced in the African land of Ham, they went to (Ps 105:23). That was one of the reasons they had to change their names in order to fit into the new culture and could become the citizens of the land of Ham. Abram changed his name by adding the HAM to his name Abram to become Abraham and that gave him citizenship, and he married an African woman by name Haggai and had children. During this time Sarai was sent to marry a man in the land and for years the man could not have a child with her, and she decided to go back to Abraham as a wife. She had to change her name from Sarai to Sarah in order to go near Abraham. When she went there, she created problem with Haggai because she had children for Abraham. She decided to submit to Abraham. She went closer to Abraham and called him Lord, to create a place in him to go to after death, with the intention to block Haggai from connecting with Abraham after death. The scripture says she had a son at old age, named Isaach, and Isaach was regarded as promised child instead of all the children Abraham had with Haggai. The Abraham-Haggai blood lineage and Abraham-Sarah blood lineage had caused a serious conflict between the Jews and the Arab still this day. This means that Abraham –Sarah lineage has no right to reign because their relationship to have a child was unholy in the land if Ham they went to. The only accepted union was Abraham and Haggai, and the distorted record must be corrected in order to solve the problem between Muslim and. The Abraham and Sarah case was brought in to show the importance of women going back into men to become whole after death. The concept of 'hell' was created by the male religious leaders for women who will not be able to get back into men to become one because it was created by Lucifer after deceiving Adam and Eve. This shows that two becoming one for heaven is for the kingdom of Lucifer-god on earth, not the kingdom of Heaven for Jesus. This means that when you are born again and receive the Spirit of Jesus, you are whole in the Spirit for Jesus, because Jesus came and restored the wholesome Spirit that Adam lost. And when your body dies, your spirit goes to Jesus in Heaven, but you must disconnect from Lucifer-god and connect to Jesus, the I AM, to prepare your spirit for Jesus. I want you to know that the lost word of I AM was restored through Angel Gabriel into Mary to solve the problem. This war is a very serious one. On June 10, 2019, at 9:50am, the Holy Spirit told me that 'homosexuality' is practiced so that men will be with men and women will be with women, in order to prevent the soul of women after death from uniting with that of men for another realm, but to stay with Lucifer-Satan-god in his kingdom on earth. This means when all men's ghosts are retained by Lucifer-Satan-god, he will have enough ghost soldiers for the David's army for Lucifer-Satan-god to go back and fight the I AM, the creator in heaven to get back his place and try to over-throw the I AM and take over the throne. Details are discussed in a separate chapter.

This process confirms that the place called hell is for female beings. This also can lead to Lesbians ghosts after death to gang up together and stand with Eve-Devil-goddess to fight Lucifer-Stan-god, and this may disrupt Lucifer's effort to go up to fight in heaven, where he was thrown out because of rebellion. I am giving you all these to get you excited to read this book, that will open your eyes. I advise you to do away with religious lies and deception, and seek spiritual understanding, in order to know the truth, and the truth will set you free from religious bondage and spiritual slavery. The worst oppressive systems in the world are 'religion and politics'

Some Christians have said that most sicknesses and diseases are spiritual and are caused by Satan. I want people to know that thousands of people who die of different diseases every year around the world, are caused by spiritual war to destroy the evil body that Adam and Eve were remade into by Lucifer after they had sinned and lost the divine nature made to live forever. Many people believe that prayer will solve the problem of sickness and death. It is good to pray, but it is important to know that Adam and Eve were divinely created to procreate gods and angels to live forever, to serve in the first level of the Kingdom of Heaven that was about to be restored to join back to the second and third heaven, but Lucifer deceived them and remade them in his own image, and it is the 'remade' evil body that death must destroy in order to release the evil human soul that came into Adam and Eve from Lucifer into a special Community in the spirit world for Lucifer-GOD. Lucifer, who has become the god of this world, has created different religions that confused people and redirected their attention to himself as god, and has created religious laws that made people to pray for their souls to go to heaven. The question is, which heaven? It is good to know that the 'kingdom of god' is different from the 'kingdom of heaven'. The kingdom of God is the 'supernatural world' within the first level of the kingdom of heaven that Lucifer and his angels occupied to serve the I AM and after he has rebelled against I AM, it was cut off from the upper levels and covered with water. The kingdom of God is owned by Lucifer who deceived Adam and became the god of this world.

The kingdom of heaven is the throne of the Creator, the I AM and of Jesus, the I AM, who came into the kingdom of God to save humanity from the sufferings created by Lucifer, the god of this world, and the kingdom of heaven includes the second and third heavens above realm now occupied by Lucifer god and the evil created human beings.

My revelation on August 3, 2018: it was about Adam and Eve procreation by the 'word' but they lost it by sinning. I was taught in the dream that Adam was created by the I AM without 'PENIS' but from the mouth. Adam's mouth was not to eat and drink because he was a divine being like angels and did not have food to eat and water to drink before he sinned, because there is no food in heaven, and the kingdom built for Adam before he sinned was made of gold, diamond and precious stones, and the light was the light of the Holy Spirit and not the sun or the fire from cooking. Adam was given power to sow the word into Eve, and Eve was given power to speak the word out to become a being as angelic being. Eve did not have sex organ 'VAGINA' for sex.

It was Lucifer, the fallen angel who created 'VAGINA' in Eve and taught her sex and both Lucifer and Eve went and created 'PENIS' in Adam and taught him how to have sex with Eve. Both Adam and Eve lost their divine nature and spirit of I AM, and Lucifer become their god and remade them in his own image by giving them his spirit called 'soul'.

The 'PENIS' that Lucifer created on himself first, to have sex with Eve is what the Bible called Serpent'(Gen 3:14). A man's penis is like a snake, and a woman's vagina is like the hidden dragon with the clitoris-tongue that directs the semen-sperm to the womb. This is why most cultures require circumcision for both male and female children when they are born. It was the change of Adam and Eve into the image of Lucifer-god that helped Lucifer to have his lineage on earth. This is an indication that 'sex' was the original sin, not the eating of the fruit as recorded in the Bible, and that sexual union established blood line for Adam and Eve and their generations to follow Lucifer as their god in this world. It was Lucifer who created the concept of marriage after he has joined Adam and Eve by sex.

The last instruction for religious people, it is the duty of women to restore the lost spiritual connection, by loving their husbands affectionately in order to connect back to their husbands by the spirit, not by their 'soul' for the restoration of one created being 'Elohim', in order to skip hell, because Eve was unfaithful and disconnected from her master Adam when she listened to Lucifer, the fallen angel. Many people have not understood Apostle Paul. In Eph 5: 21-23, Paul presents two concepts of 'submit and respect' to wives and presents one concept of 'love' to the husbands, and instructs them to produce words of love out of their mouths to wash their wives like water. The love for only the husbands and not the wives, has left a vacuum for connection. A wife that does not produce any word of love back to her husband, but only takes words of love from her husband and tries to submit and respect, does not try to prepare a place in her husband to go back to after death, will end up in hell.

In I Cor7:39-40, the scripture says that a woman is bound to her husband as long as he lives, and if he dies, she can marry anyone she wishes, but she be happier if she stays unmarried after her husband's death. Many people may not understand what Paul says, and that has resulted in a lot of marital problems for millions of years.

Here Apostle Paul instructs a woman to marry one man as long as he lives, and if he dies, the woman should remain without another husband. This is clear that one woman will return to one man after death, and if she married two men, she will not be able to divide into two for the two men, but must develop strong love for one of the two men or she will Go to hell because she is now a redundant individual after death, who did not have affection for one and a particular man-husband while alive in the natural world. A man can marry more than one wife, but only one of those wives that had a strong and powerful 'affection-energy' for the man will go back into the man by the spirit, not the soul. Finally, I want to remind both male and female, husband and wife that connection to become 'Elohim' again as an angel, both husband and wife must be born of the spirit, and to be born of the spirit both husband and wife must crucify and disconnect from the human soul in them, and then connect with the Spirit of Jesus. This will be discussed in a book by itself, but just a hint, if a person does not disconnect from the human 'soul' that came from Lucifer to Adam and Eve during deception, no wife will be able to connect back to the husband in this spirit to form the 'Elohim' and connect with Jesus.

All the born again taught in churches and other religious organizations with human soul alive, is building up the kingdom of GOD with human, soul that people pray to become Christ. This is purely a kingdom built for Lucifer, the god of this world. This is the kingdom of God, which is different from the kingdom of heaven, the throne of Jesus.

Another very important point is 'skin color-racism'. It is the dark brown called 'black' that is causing all the problems of 'racism'. It is important to know that every human being has 'light brown' color called 'white'.

If an African looks at his/her palm and under his/her feet, the person will see that the palm and under the feet retain the original color.

Listen: the dark brown color that covers the rest of the body is 'identity' to differentiate the Adamic-Hamitic-Canaanite-African race being the original created race by the I AM, the Creator, from the luciferian-shemitic-caucisian racial group, that evolved through Lucifer's sexual union with Eve.

I want Africans to know that there is nothing wrong with the color of your skin as people label it black and evil. The color makes you special as the created being while others evolved through adultery and immoral sexual union and intermarriage. All non-African racial groups know about it, except Africans who have refused to see the truth. This is why the Luciferian racial groups developed different religions that made Africans to be easily disconnected from the I AM, their Creator, to their god, Lucifer the fallen angel, and they have succeeded in keeping them to their God until this day. The sad part of it is that they kept the secret to themselves and introduced the fake part of their religion to the Africans, who have prayed, fasted but nothing good has happened to them until this day. The other reason is that the day that Lucifer defeated Eve, the goddess and pushed her into the bottom of the kingdom of the sea, the African mind was locked into their body as a prison, and they are unable to speak out against the fake religion that does not work for them till this day.

On April 11, 2019, I had a dream, in which I was with a group of people, and the only discussion for the whole night was 'the human mind must be cleaned up of all the lies, distorted and false information for it to receive the truth'. This means that human mind has been filled with junks and there is no space for the truth. The junks are about what John 5: 39-40 states that the Jews studied the scriptures and prophesy by the Prophets but did not know the one the prophets talked about. Those who listened to Jesus did not know him because they referred their mind to what the dead had said about him, instead of listening to the one that was talked about, who was in front of them. This means that we study the work of the dead, the Old Testament, instead of receiving from the Holy Spirit. In John 21:25, the scripture says that if all the work done by Jesus were to be written down, the whole world cannot contain all the books. This tells us that we have about 1% of what Jesus did, and the 99% that was not written down or destroyed must be received from the Holy Spirit. This is the Holy Spirit era, and we must do away with the work of the dead. This is a very interesting book, please enjoy reading the whole book.

I am ending this inspirational introduction with a very important point. Wars, fights and violence do not intend to spare life. The fighters' intention is to conquer and possess to dominate and rule. If Lucifer-god and Eve-goddess are fighting, as discussed in different chapters, their intentions cannot produce peace, harmony and love. This then means that any good word, sign, blessings and pronouncement you see in the Bible and other religious books, came from Jesus, the I AM, who came as the Mediator, Redeemer and Savior, for the suffering, who are caught up in the wars, fights and violence produced by these two fighters. This is the misunderstanding that people have in differentiating the laws of God or be punished, without the goddess in the scene from the mercy and the grace of Jesus, the I AM. The goddess will continue to fight, because people are turning to God, without mentioning the goddess. The more you call on God, the more you have problems in this world, because the Goddess who is left out will continue to fight.

I was sent into this world to restore the truth that Jesus taught, but was distorted in order to give credit to Lucifer, the god of this world. Forces have fought me for more than twenty years. For example, in 2002, my Lord Jesus, the I AM asked me to go and raise an altar in Africa to destroy the power of witchcraft that has kept African race at the bottom of the universe for billions of years. I went to Akwa Ibom state in Nigeria, and bought a land to lay the altar. I stood on the land and after I had set up the altar in the ground, and was bout to make the pronouncements, I was slapped by the invisible hand, and I fell down on the ground for about twenty to twenty five minutes. Those who were with me prayed until I got up. Finally, I got up and completed laying the altar, evil forces that fought me continues. The person who was given the contract to build the building, built it without a roof, and took the money and built his house in the village and bought two cars, one for him and one for his wife.

Finally today, people have built houses around the building with no road to get to where the altar was laid. The truth to the world is, the fight between Lucifer-god and Eve –goddess will continue until the planet earth is closed down, unless we disconnect from God and goddess, and connect only with Jesus, the I AM, to restore our relationship with this truth, we are doomed to fail with the present religious counseling that prepares our souls for the kingdom of God. Get into the whole book and share with others.

CHAPTER TWO

The Great I AM: The Truth and Freedom from Religious Bondage and Spiritual Slavery

I begin my writing with the command given to Moses in the midst of the bush, where he spent 40 years crying and praying out of love for his people and his desire to find solution to the sufferings of his people, as recorded in (Exo 3:14-15). The 'Voice' by the power of the 'word' told Moses to tell his people that as from that moment he received the 'word' that his name as I AM must be kept forever and must be his memorial to all generations. Here, the supreme Creator told Moses to drop the title 'God' and present his real name I AM as his memorial to all generations. According to the Webster's New World Dictionary (1992), memorial means helping people to remember some person. This means that the I AM commanded Moses to write the name down in order to teach his people and remind them to pass it on from generation to generation.

A sacrifice could be made in every generation to remind the people of the name of their Creator as the I AM (Is 66: 3). The instruction given to Moses was the permanent historical record that had to be kept in all generations.

The name if the Creator I AM was dropped immediately Lucifer deceived Adam and became the God of this world, and religious were created to project the name 'God' that hid the name Lucifer, the fallen angel who became the angel of light and everyone followed him.

It is important to know that scientific and anthropological researches concluded that human beings started in Africa. If the I AM created 'Man' in his own image, it means that 'Man' then 'Adam' had the nature and spirit of the I AM, and if 'Man-Adam' was the first being created by the I AM, then it confirms that the I AM, the Creator is an African. This then shows that the Jews, Israelites, Europeans and Arabs disconnected African Race from their Creator, the I AM, and connected the Africans to their God and established their religions and connect back to their Creator, the I AM, by starting their own spiritual truth that I call 'Jesiamism' with direct connection to Jesus, the I AM.

The Bible gives wrong information that Moses was a Jew. Moses was African, and in his heart broken for his people's suffering, he journeyed to find solution for his fellow Africans in slavery, the I AM revealed himself to him and gave Moses power and guidelines on how to get his people out of slavery.

It is a big mistake for people to write that the Creator who revealed his name as 'I AM', also revealed his name as God. The I AM knew that people presented God, the created being to take his position because I AM, the Creator has direct connection with his first created African race, and they gave different names of God to cover up the name if the Creator, I AM. The I AM is the self created being, who created the generation of beings into existence (Is 41:4). The I AM is the supreme being and he is limited to his throne in the heavenly realm. He has no relationship with this universe, except through his 'word' that he sent out to become 'Jesus' who came into this universe as the revealed I AM, and when he came, he restored the lost/ hidden name of the Creator I AM (Exo 3:14-15; John 8:58)

The I AM, whose name was changed to be 'Yahweh' by the Jews, in order to disconnect the direct line from I AM to the African Race as revealed to Moses, who was an African, sent by the I AM reconnect him back to his original creation. The I AM did that to show that he is the supreme Creator, who existed as an Independent and only divine being. The Jews refused to acknowledge I AM as the Creator because of the African origin.

The scripture says that before the earth was formed and man was created, was the I AM (Ps 90:2). This shows that the I AM, the Creator existed before he created the earth and then 'man-Adam-god' on earth.

In Ps 105: 11; 23;25; 27, the scripture tells is that before 'Abram' went to the land of 'Ham', that is the ;and of Egypt in Africa, and intermarried became a citizen of Egypt in Africa, and then changed his name from 'Abram' to 'Abra-Ham' or 'Abraham' in order to become a part of the Hamitic system, the I AM was already there. The I AM was the Creator of the Hamitic-African race before Abraham was born. The statement by Jesus in John 8: 58; is intended to express the relationship with the I AM, the Creator, and Jesus as the revealed I AM, to confirm the statement in Ps 90: 2, that before the earth was formed the Creator, I AM was. The Creator I AM, is the only Great Source of life, love, light and has passed these qualities to Jesus, the revealed I AM. The Greta I AM created life and he does not take life and Jesus came into the world and passed through all the sufferings without taking any life. It is an insult for people or religions to equate any being they call 'God' that steals, judges, enslaves, oppresses and kills, while the I AM creates life and does not take life.

The I AM is not the God of Abraham, Jacob, and Isaack who destroyed the Canaanites and helped the Abraham's generations to claim another people's land and property. The I AM is the Creator of life and does not take life. He stays only in the heavenly realm. There is only one heavenly realm with three levels, and this is different from the religious heaven for God that is 'Supernatural realm' simply means spirit world or the world or the world of the dead, that belongs to Lucifer=god who deceived Adam and Eve to bring death to humanity. This supernatural realm is of this natural world and has no connection to the heavenly realm, the throne of I AM and Jesus, the I AM.

The problem that still exist, is that people have been confused to take the name I AM as one of the Gods, instead of regarding him as the one and only Creator while those they called God and gods were created by the I AM, even Lucifer who is the God of this world was created by the I AM as angel in the heavenly realm, but was driven out when he rebelled against his Creator.

I did a research to find out how the name I AM can mean Yahweh, Jehovah, Adonai, and discovered that in Hebrew language, Ehyeh, Yahweh were translated as I AM, meaning that the I AM was translate into the names of local deities. There is only one language in the world that meets the name I AM as it is without changing any of the alphabets. That language is spoken by one of the smallest tribe called 'Ibibio' of Akwa Ibom state in Nigeria, West Africa. The name of the Creator is I AM and the Ibibio language word is AMI. AMI means I AM. The I AM means AMI. This is the only direct translation of the I AM, and does not replace it with any local god, deity or a different letter.

When Jesus came, he revealed himself as I AM (John 8:58). There is no 'J' in Ibibio language, but 'Y' and the name Jesus is written as Yesus. To connect I AM with Jesus, the I AM as one creator, I put the two Ibibio words together to form AMIYESU, as the Almighty Creator. This is the name of our Creator, particularly the African race.

It is very sad to see that all the instructions the I AM gave to Moses to redirect his people, were rewritten and turned into synagogue of Satan to show Lucifer as the god in the Old Testament, and into the world of war between Lucifer's spirit-Satan and the Eve's spirit-devil. The Bible writers either destroyed or ignored the work of I AM because it was connected with the enslaved African race. From Genesis to Malachi, the scripture portrays wars, violence, destruction enslavement, oppression, exploitation, murder, genocide and all forms of evil activities. These make human beings to fight among themselves, not knowing that all these are caused by the war between Lucifer and Eve.

The title of 'God' that Adam lost to Lucifer during deception is now redundant because Lucifer has come out openly now by sending his spirit-Satan to rule the world through different organizations as church of Satan, synagogue of Satan.

Satanic temple, satanic beast system, Luciferian priesthood etc, it is heartbroken to see that all religions in the world have their foundations on what Lucifer-god has set up as the Almighty God and Creator, but he hid from the public, the information that their individual deities acts as their gods, but answer to Lucifer-Satan as the Almighty god.

When Jesus came, he revealed himself as the I AM (John 8:58), not as god. Fake Jesus, called Christ, was brought in as the son of god, to sacrifice for human sins, but did not tell us which of the thousands of god was his father.

Lucifer, the god of this world has set up his kingdom of heaven and hell in this universe but has allowed the positions for god to be vacant, because all the problems in the world are blamed on him as one who has no power to solve them. As god, he is facing a very tough war Eve, the Goddess which is very difficult to win, this is why the word god is not workings anymore, and even the Jews write G-D without the 'O' meaning 'OVER'.

This is why people and their prayers and other request to God with the name 'Jesus' and although the fake word 'Christ' was attached to the name Jesus, Jesus answers those prayers because of love he got from the Creator of life, the I AM.

<u>Fig 1</u>
<u>The I AM – Creator and His Heavenly Psalm.</u>
<u>The Heavely Realm has three levels of 1,2,3,</u>
<u>The Home of Angels</u>

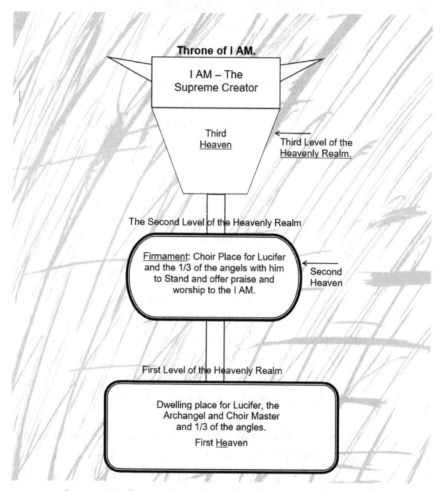

Source: Understanding the Bile and Creation (2007:62)

This diagram in fig one represents the heavenly realm created by I AM, the Creator, and this might have existed for billions of years as the home of angels, without the presence or knowledge of a being called god or man.

There was nothing in existence as 'human' characteristics of the kingdom of heaven.

The I AM created the heavenly realm and created angels to serve in the heavenly realm. The angels were given the 'laws of love', and that produced the atmosphere of peace, harmony and blessings to all the creation in heaven. The angelic population was divided into two groups.

The first group of two third of the entire population served in the third heaven, the throne of I AM under the leadership of the Archangel Lucifer, to serve at the first heavenly realm. The second heaven was/is a platform for Lucifer and his choir to stand and minister praise and worship to the Creator, I AM. All the three divisions of heavenly realm were governed by the laws of 'love, peace, harmony, holiness, perfection and life' set for the angels.

The angles were/are spirit beings without a soul are walking in the power of light, which is the nature of the heavenly realm of the Great I AM.

The Great I AM created the angels and put his nature of light and love in them to love one another and have peace and harmony to maintain the atmosphere of the heavenly realm.

The law of love and the command to love, are the perfect principle that the angels live with in the heavenly realm or the kingdom of heaven. This shows that love is the perfect source by which to live a 'life'. The kingdom of heaven or heavenly realm for angels is charged with the power of love, and the law of love expresses itself in peace, harmony and perfection and that affects the mind of the angels and controls it.

The I AM is self existed being who was aware of himself, and had the conscious need to create the angelic beings to form the community and relational love, and he called himself I AM, because he created himself, and also created angels to relate with him. After he has created the heavenly kingdom with all the angels, he ten introduced himself to the angels as I AM. He then created the spirit being called 'Love' and allowed the love to empower them and unite them as one.

The ancient name of the Creator in Ibibio language, a small tribe in the south eastern part of Nigeria, West African is I AM. 'AMI' means 'I

AM' the Creator of the heavenly kingdom and the angels. He is one with no beginning. This name 'AMI' refers to 'Individual' who is self created supreme being, without reference to another name or being.

The Creator whose name is AMI, or I AM and the angels, are divine and all knew everything and live in the divine realm that correspond to the concepts of Omnipotent, Omnipresent, Omniscience and Omnisient. The entire hosts of heaven are created to live by the direction of the Holy Spirit of I AM. The kingdom of heaven was built with gold and is beautiful with pearls (Matt13:45) and the created angels live eternal life in the heavenly realm (John 1:2).

The I AM created the power of the Holy love to rule over the entire kingdom of heaven, and it allowed the I AM to love all the angels and the angels love one another as the I AM loves them (John 15:12). The kingdom of heaven flows with wisdom and generates purity, peace, gentleness and mercy (John 3:17). Another characteristic of the kingdom of heaven is eternal life and it allows the angels to experience glory, honor and immortality, unity and harmony, and are full of wisdom to stay perfect (Matt 5:44-45) and they remain perfect in one as they share in the same life of the holy love (John 17:22-23), to produce joy, peace, kindness, faithfulness and self control (Gal 5:22-23).

The kingdom of heaven is the abode of the Great I AM, the supreme Creator, and of Jesus, the I AM, and of the holy angels, above the universe. The original created heavenly realm contained three divine and holy divisions.

The first heaven for Lucifer, the archangel and his angels, the second heaven is the firmament as a platform for choir and music ministration to the I AM. The third heaven is the throne of the I AM, the Supreme Creator and the angels serving.

It is important to know that the heavenly realm or the kingdom of the heaven is the spiritual realm that is above the universe that human beings live now, and it is invisible realm for holy angels who are serving at the throne of the Great I AM. Some people write books of how they spent some time in heaven with Jesus, Jesus says in John 3:13 that no one has been to heaven except he that came from there and went back. This means that only Jesus who came from the I AM, by the spoken 'word' through angel Gabriel into Mary who rose from the death is the only one in heaven with the angels.

Any human beings who was conceived by the human 'SPERM' who lived and died without resurrection cannot go to heaven. The church has deceived people with the scripture that was written at the beginning of the created beings, the 'man' and Adam-god and Lucifer-god with the exclusion of the I AM the supreme Creator. The details of man and Adam's work was excluded and the entire Old Testament contains the work of Lucifer as god of this world.

People make mistake of seeing the supernatural realm as heaven. The supernatural realm is the celestial map of the universe and the planets. It is the place for the ancestral gods, the ghosts of the dead, located above the natural or physical realm particularly for the souls of men after death. The sun, moon, planets, stars, etc are found in the supernatural realm, invisible to human eyes, but both natural and supernatural are in this universe, below the second level of the kingdom if heaven, separated by a boundary that keeps the universe in the first level of the kingdom of heaven that is now this world ruled by Lucifer-god and it is not connected to the upper level, the kingdom of heaven of the Great I AM and of Jesus, the I AM.

The angelic realm with the I AM the supreme Creator might have existed for billions of years before Lucifer rebelled against the I AM and the heavenly realm was restructured as shown in Fig 2

Fig 2.
Rebellion in Heaven and the Restruction – Division of Heaven

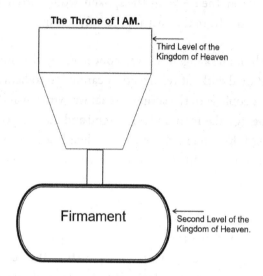

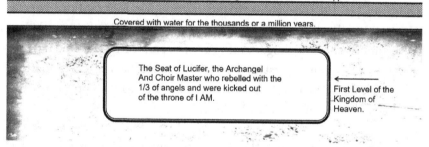

Figure 2: Lucifer rebelled against the I AM and he was kicked out of heaven

In figure 2, the diagram shows that Lucifer the archangel, who was the choir master for the one-third of the angels rebelled against the I AM and wanted to take his throne to be worshipped by the angels, instead of him leading the angels to offer praise and worship to the I AM, the Supreme Creator. There was war in heaven and angel Michael and his group of angels defeated Lucifer and his group and after sending him and the one third of the angels to the first level of the kingdom of heaven. The place was covered with water and boundary was created to separate the first level of the kingdom of heaven from the throne of I AM, and it was left to stay under the water for thousands or a million years. The only punishment was to lock Lucifer into the body of a lower being called 'beast' and all the angels with him were also locked into the body of lower beings as sea creatures and mammals (Mbosowo 2007).

After thousands or a million years, the I AM revisited the abandoned area, with the intention to rebuild the first level of the kingdom of heaven to connect back to the upper level of the throne of I AM.

The rebuilding of the lost first level of the kingdom of heaven is shown in fig 3

Fig 3.
Revisitation of the abandoned first level of the kingdom of heaven

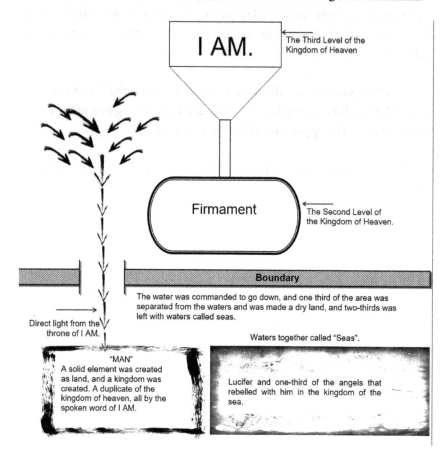

Fig 3: the I AM revisited the abandoned first level of heaven

The I AM revisited the abandoned first level of heaven. He commanded the water to go down to the proper level and created a solid element called land and built the supplicate of the kingdom of heaven on one third of the place and allowed two third to remain as the body of waters called seas because Lucifer and one third of angels that became the kingdom of the sea for them as sea creatures and mammals, to continue their lives, since the I AM is the Creator of life and does not destroy life. Lucifer, the fallen angel was locked into the body of a lower being called 'beast' and even though he was walking around like a being, he was not given the ability to speak for thousands of years after he has deceived Adam and Eve. In Rev 20: 7, the scripture says that after the thousand years Satan will be released out of prison.

Most people misunderstand this scripture to mean that Satan will be let out of prison as a building. Lucifer was angelic spirit being. After he rebelled against I AM and was kicked out, he remained in the body of water for thousands of years and for him to function well in water, he was locked into the body of a beast a sea animal, and was unable to speak. He must have have had a way of communicating with the angels who were also locked into the body of sea creatures, and they were given the kingdom of the sea as their dwelling place.

The I AM created, the angelic being called "Man" to control the restored first level of the kingdom of heaven built on the one third of the place beside the kingdom of the sea, with the authority to rule both the restored first level of the kingdom of heaven and the kingdom of the sea (Mbosowo 2007) the reign and the activities of the 'man' that are not found in the Bible, are discussed in Chapter 4.

I waited to discuss the concepts of 'Religions Bondage and the Spiritual Slavery'.

CHAPTER THREE

The Creation of 'Man' – The Missing Link

Lucifer, the archangel who rebelled against I AM, the Creator in heaven, and there was war between the army of the I AM led by Angel Michael and Lucifer with the one third of the angels that rebelled with him, and Lucifer was defeated and was locked out of the third heaven, and was restricted to the first level of the heavenly realm, and a demarcation was created between the lower level of the heaven realm where Lucifer was and the upper level of the heavenly realm, and the lower level of the heavenly realm was covered with water, and the Spirit of the I AM was hovering over the face of the waters (Gen 1:2). This is what the Bible does not record. When Lucifer was thrown out of heaven, he was locked into the body of a lower being called 'beast', and he promised to make sure that all the beings that will be created to occupy the first level of the heavenly realm will rebel against authority and be locked into a body like him. This is what he did to the angels created by the 'man' and 'Adam'.

The waters had covered the lower level of the heavenly realm with Lucifer and his angels for thousands of years. This is what the scripture talks about in Gen 1:2 as 'the earth was on the face of the deep'. All these processes were the thousands of years that Lucifer and his angels lived in the deep of waters before the I AM revisited the dark area. This is the missing link in the Bible that has given human beings wrong information about creation.

After thousands of years, I AM visited the lower part of the heavenly realm with waters. In Gen 1:9-10, the scripture says 'let the waters under the heavens be gathered together into one place, and let the dry land appear, and it was so' and the dry land was called 'Earth' and the gatherings together of the waters, he called seas…'

This scripture does not give us the true picture of what happened to the lower level of the heavenly realm given to Lucifer as the archangel and his angels, and how it was separated from the upper level of the heavenly realm and was covered with water when Lucifer rebelled against the I AM, the Creator.

I am presenting the true picture here. After the first level of heavenly realm was covered with waters for thousands a=of years, the Creator I AM revisited the area. In the deep sea, that is a kingdom itself, Lucifer, the rebellious angel was locked into the body of a 'beast' and all his angels were also locked into the body of the sea creatures and mammals as punishment. Because the sea has become the kingdom for the rebellious angels, the Creator separated the waters from the boundary to the level we see now as oceans and rivers. He then made one third of the mass water dry and called it land. He built back the first level of the heavenly realm with gold and all kinds of precious stones as the restoration of the of the first level of the heavenly realm, and as the duplicate of the heavenly realm. This shows that the word "Land" with sand element has nothing to do with the foundation on which the first level of the kingdom of heaven was built.

That was done to restore what Lucifer, the rebel had destroyed, so that the heavenly realm would go back to the three stages with angelic beings at the first level taking up the duty of coming up to the second level of the realm to praise and worship I AM, the Creator.

After the first level of the heavenly realm was restored, the scripture in Gen 1:27 says: 'the I AM created 'Man' in his own image, in image of I AM created he 'HIM' male and female created he them. The I AM blessed them and said to them 'be fruitful and multiply, fill the earth and subdue it'.

When the I AM created 'MAN' in his own image, the 'MAN' was the Spirit of the I AM that he spoke by his 'word' into being, and the 'MAN' was created with two functions of 'MALE' and 'FEMALE', as the compound power for creation. He was the 'Elohim' and had the power to speak beings out of him into existence. The Bible does not mention what 'MAN' did and how many years he lived and ruled the kingdom.

Man and his creation

After the 'Man-angelic-spirit' of the I AM was created as the head of the restored first level of heavenly realm, he created angels as the messengers to serve in the kingdom because he was blessed with the power to produce and multiply. This restored the first level of the kingdom of heaven that did not have trees, grass or any of the objects that we see in this world, just because it was purely the duplicate of the heavenly structure for the 'MAN'. You cannot find this in the Bible.

It is important to know that all what I AM has done was by spoken words. What I am going to say is what I received from a teaching seminar in the DREAM, and when I woke up, it was confirmed to me by the holy spirit. All the animals that we see today were originally angelic beings that the 'MAN' created to serve in the kingdom, and to restore the choir to go up and worship the I AM, and I believe that the tradition that was disrupted by Lucifer might have going on for generations because of different kinds of animals that we have today. It was Lucifer who was locked into a beast that corrupted those angels to rebel against 'MAN', and all the angels who rebelled were locked into the body of lower beings called animal.

For example, there are so many kinds of animals, but I decided to mention only a few, such as bear, deer, dog, cat, cattle, elephant, goat, giraffe, goose, hippopotamus, leopard. Lizard, lion, monkey, pigs, rabbits, chimpanzee, gorilla, squirrel, tiger, turtle, wolf, foxes. Each of these groups of animals represent a generation of the angels created by 'MAN' to inhabit the kingdom and served 'MAN', as the representative of I AM, and for the 'MAN' to act as the choir master and take the angels to the second heaven to praise and worship the Creator as Lucifer did with the one third of the angels before be rebelled against the I AM, the Creator and was kicked out of heaven.

Lucifer was in the kingdom of the sea as locked into the body of a 'beast', with all the angels that rebelled with him also locked into different bodies of sea creatures. He realized that 'MAN' had restored the choir with his angels and had been going up to the second heaven to praise and worship the I AM, the Creator. Lucifer decided to go after those angels with 'MAN' he succeeded to corrupt them, and those angels rebelled against the 'MAN' and all of them were locked into the body of lower beings called animals. It is important to know that Lucifer who was locked into the body of a 'beast' is still walking around as a 'beast' till today, and he uses his spirit-satan to rule the world. He promised that no spirit being will be free to walk around, and he made the human soul to be locked into the body called 'HU' that allows man to be in prison of body or house. This will be discussed in detail in the later chapters.

The different types of animal I have mentioned, show that at least twenty generations of twenty thousand or millions of years were the period ruled by 'MAN' before Lucifer was at the point of almost bringing down the 'MAN' after he has corrupted all the angels in those generations created by 'MAN'. Lucifer was not happy because 'MAN' was given authority to rule him and every creature in the kingdom of the sea. The creation of 'MAN' and his ruling of the kingdom for at least twenty thousand or millions of years had not been mentioned in the Bible. Lucifer succeeded in making those angels rebel against 'MAN' in those generations, and all the angels were locked into the body of lower beings called animals, and Lucifer was happy because all his angels were locked into the sea creatures.

The channel of communication was taken away from the animals so that they could not tell human anything about their generations. This is why animals cannot speak. Lucifer continues to deceive and prevent human beings from knowing to truth until this day, and though human beings are still locked into the body as prison until after death, and it is good to know that human beings are praising and worshiping Lucifer as the god of this world.

Making of animals and languages

The Great I AM is the Creator and giver of life and he does not destroy life. That was why all the angels who rebel against authority were locked into the body of lower beings. People make mistake to see I AM as God, and say that god gave life and god takes life. Lucifer is the god the this world and he gives life through 'human sperm' and takes life but the I AM who created angels through spoken 'word' does not take life. More on this is discussed in the next chapter.

Dog: these beings must have served faithfully for too long. This must be why dogs are the best pets to human. This generation-being-dogs must have existed for a million years before they were corrupted by Lucifer and were locked into the body of lower being called dog. The sound of this being could be heard in different languages:

1- French: WAOUH
2- Russian: GAV
3- Spanish: GVAV
4- Dutch: BLAF
5- Japanese: WAN
6- Italian: BAU
7- Korean: MEONG
8- Persian: HAAP
9- Turkish: HEV
10- English: WOOF

CAT:

1- Swedish: MJAU
2- Russian: MYAU
3- Spanish: MIAU
4- English: MEOW
5- French: MIAOU

PIGS:

This generation of beings might have served 'MAN' for a million years before Lucifer was able to corrupt them, and after they had been locked into the body of animal called 'pig'. Their ability to speak was taken away but their language sounds are known to human beings today as

1- English: OINK
2- 2-Japanese BUU
3- Germany: GRUNZ
4- Swedish: NOFF
5- Dutch: KNOR

HORSE:

1- English: NEIGH
2- Japanese: HIHIIN
3- Swedish: GNAGG
4- Russian: I-GO-GO
5- Polish: I –HAAAAA

Animal kingdom has been set up in movies, home pets, Disney and action plays by human beings without knowing the creation, foundation and the generations of the beings we call animals. After Lucifer has tempted the 'MAN' for millions of years through generations in the kingdom, and was about to make him fall, so that he could disrupt the choir restored by 'MAN' to continue the worship of I AM, the Creator, the I AM stepped in with a different level of creation.

In gen 2:7, the scripture says 'and the I AM formed 'MAN' of the dust of the ground and breathed into his nostrils the breath of life, and the 'MAN' became a living being.

I have already stated that the kingdom for 'MAN' was made of gold, diamond, and precious stones as the restoration of the first level of heavenly realm disrupted by Lucifer. For this reason, the word 'dust' should not be here until after Adam had sinned and went to build his physical world that we live in now. This means that the substance was divine element like gold. This must be why most religions use gold money as the symbol stature of their gods to represent material world.

To compare the scripture in Gen 1:27
-So I AM created 'MAN' in his own image with the scripture in gen 2:7 'And I AM formed 'MAN' of the dust of the ground...' shows two different creations that the Bible does not explain.

This is my explanation:

The first 'MAN' created in the image of I AM, was an angel-spirit being to take the place that Lucifer was thrown out, while the second 'MAN' was not really a being, rather a substance that was created as a house-body system, after the 'MAN' who ruled the kingdom for millions of years, and was about to be defeated by Lucifer, was put inside the substance, and the substance became a living being, called body (Mbosowo 2007).

This is the work that the 'MAN' did for a million years and how Lucifer, the fallen angel continued to fight, and succeeded in getting all the angels who served 'MAN' to rebel and be locked into the body of lower beings called animals, as he is in the body of the beast.

After Lucifer was locked into the body of a beast, he promised that every angelic being will be locked into a body as prison like him. He was so much after 'MAN' created by the I AM to rule the restored first kingdom of heaven, and before he succeeded, the I AM created a protected being for the 'MAN' called Adam. The creation of Adam and his activities that are not in the Bible are discussed in chapter 4.

The picture here shows that all the angels created by 'MAN' to serve, who were corrupted by Lucifer to rebel against 'MAN' were all locked into the body of lower beings and all of them were walking around like human, but were controlled by cage called body, and were not allowed to speak till this day.

The animals were subjected to walking on four feet by Lucifer after he has succeeded in getting the created human soul locked into the body as prison. It is sad that human beings do not know that after Lucifer had deceived Adam and Eve, and allowed the spermatic procreated beings locked into the body to speak, was for those called 'human' to have a voice to praise and worship him as their god, and this has been on for millions of years without people knowing the truth till this day.

CHAPTER FOUR

Creation of Adam – Missing Link

It was the living substance that was called 'ADAM' and inside 'ADAM' was only the spirit of I AM called 'MAN'. Adam was now in existence as a being with the responsibility of caring and protecting the 'MAN' in him. Adam now became the mouth through him that the 'MAN' in him speaks. The scripture in Gen 2: 19-29 says that 'the beast and birds were formed out of the ground and brought them to Adam to give names'. This scripture does not fit with the nature of the kingdom that the I AM built with gold and precious stones for 'MAN' and was about to put Adam into it. The structure and nature of the duplicated kingdom of heaven for 'MAN' did not have a ground for vegetation until Adam sinned and was driven out to build his natural world not with 'word' because he lost it, but 'labor' for human suffering.

After Adam was made as the protector of 'MAN' he was given the title 'God' by the I AM and all the angelic-animal-beings who were still walking straight were brought to Adam to name them. It was through Adam that the concept of 'god' came to be. This means that all the beings called animals were still serving in the kingdom at the lower nature in the body called animal. This means that after human beings were created and they sinned through Lucifer, Lucifer then reduced the animals to the level of surrender by walking on four legs in order to be under the authority of human beings that carry his own spirit called 'soul'.

Adam was given authority to rule both the kingdom given to him by the I AM and the kingdom of the sea where Lucifer was.

At this point Adam was carrying in him the 'MAN' with the two functions of creation (male and female) and the title "god' given to him was to show him as the 'being' who was to become the creator, god the father, the protector of the gods he would create, but the Bible does not present to work of Adam as the first god of the kingdom. I received that Adam as god, ruled the kingdom for thousands of years before he was given a female helper. Adam created his angels to serve and go up to worship I AM, the Creator, but Lucifer also corrupted those angels and they rebelled against Adam and Adam became lonely. That was the fulfillment of the promise that Lucifer made to make sure that beings on earth rebel and be locked into the body of animal as he is. All created angelic beings by 'MAN' and Adam were easily deceived and corrupted by Lucifer, but he was unable to bring down 'Adam' because he was god with glorious body with divine spirit and at this point Adam became lonely, and in Gen 2:18, the scripture says: 'The I AM saw that it was not good for the Adam-'MAN' to be alone and promise to give Adam a helper of the same nature as he is. The scripture is Gen 2:21 says that Adam was put to sleep and a rib was removed from him and made him a woman.

I want to explain here that after the spiritual surgery was done in Adam, he lost the womb and the status of 'Elohim' given to him, and now 'ELO=female' goes to the woman, and Him-Male was for Adam and he kept his title God, but the 'male' goes with Adam-MAN, while female goes with Eve-Woman.

This now shows dual nature for both Adam and Eve. Adam carries 'MAN' while Eve carried Woman-womb of a man. Although Adam and Eve were created with dual nature to make it difficult for Lucifer to mess them up, Lucifer also used his dual nature of beast and his spirit-satan to make it easier for him to deceive Adam and Eve (Mbosowo 2007).

Method of procreation by Adam and Eve

> After the two beings Adam and Eve were created by the I AM, they were given the power and method of procreating gods for the kingdom. Adam was given the power of the spoken 'word' into being and Eve was to receive the word into her in order for the word being' to have divine shelter (egg) in the body to become created before she speaks the word out into beings as angels or gods. The word was first formed in the Adam-man-spirit of the I AM in him, and he was to release the 'word' by the language given into the woman and Eve had the power and language to speak the word into the physical beings as gods to occupy the kingdom.

Lucifer knew that he would not be able to get to the 'MAN-spirit' of the I AM in Adam, he then started with Eve, with the plan to contaminate her and set her up against Adam, to bring him down for lucifer to take over. Lucifer first transformed himself by creating a 'PENIS' on himself and then he created a female sex organ on Eve, and used his 'PENIS' that looked like snake and started to teach Eve sexual intercourse. After Eve was completely satisfied and enjoyed the sexual union with Lucifer, a bargain was made between Lucifer and Eve in order to visit Adam for the same process.

Agreement:

It is deception, for the scriptures in Gen 3:1-6 to talk about serpent as the deceiver, in an effort to hide the name Lucifer who used his created PENIS that looked like snake and taught Eve sexual intercourse.

It was here that Lucifer promised Eve that if she agreed to listen to him, she would not die, rather she would be like god and she would know good and evil (Gen 2"5). She agreed and after she was remade in the image of Lucifer, she went to Adam and convinced him to have sex in order to have the same experience. Adam agreed and Lucifer went in and created a male organ 'PENIS' in Adam, and he was taught how to have sex with Eve. Both Adam and Eve lost the spirit of the I AM and received the spirit of Lucifer, and the divine method of speaking the 'word' for procreation was lost, and the method of procreation turned into sexual intercourse for man to sow 'SPERM' into the woman's womb through 'VAGINA', to be delivered physically into a being through spermatic procreation.

Religious have tried to make amends to the destroyed divine system of procreation by making women to be virgin before marriage and making men have circumcision in order to change the snake image of the PENIS. None of all these religious rules can bring back the lost divine system of the 'spoken word' into beings.

The symbol of snake and serpent became the religious sacred trees, and the sexual fruits have destroyed humanity, particularity men till this day.

The scripture says love your wife and die for her as Christ died for the church Eph 5:25.

I have not read in any record where husbands wanted to die for their wives. Let me tell you the meaning of this scripture. I think it means that husbands must love their wives sexually, and the frequent sexual intercourse with the wives will deplete them of their SPERM that is their lives, and die, while their wives who received the 'SPERM' into themselves will add life to themselves and live long. Statistics show that 13 billion husbands as compared to 1 billion wives have died worldwide. This is the secret sin of human soul that the world does not know. These two beings, the snake=MAN=PENIS and the serpent –'woman-VAGINA' are the channel of producing evil beings into the world for Lucifer the god of this world.

It is very important to know that the command that a husband should love his wife, and a wife to respect her husband means that Eve was given to Adam as a helper suitable for him (Gen 2:180, not as a wife, but as a 'worker-womb" that was taken out of him, to help Adam procreate beings with a different covering that would block Lucifer from a direct contact with them. Eve was not given a command to love Adam, but to respect him as her master, because there was no concept of 'marriage' until Lucifer deceived Eve and Adam and then joined them together through sexual union, that resulted in the concept of 'Marriage'. Even though Adam and Eve were joined as husband and wife after they had sinned and turned to Lucifer as their god, a woman was not commanded to love, and this shows the absent of the word 'love' in women. This indicates that because the word 'love' does not exist in women, they do not have 'affection' that is the spirit of 'LOVE'. It started with Eve's 'love' for Lucifer and that has turned around a woman's love for her husband to another man, which is the concepts of 'Lust and Adultery'.

This is why many marriages do not last, because most wives do not and cannot produce love for their husbands, since the word 'LOVE' is not there in them for their husband, except 'respect'. It was Lucifer who first had a physical sexual union with Eve, and that created a married union, and Lucifer was the first person that Eve developed love for before any close relationship with Adam.

The Bible says "therefore shall a man leave his father and his mother, and shall cleave unto his wife, and they shall be one flesh (Gen 2:24).

;This scripture means that after Eve had sexual union with Lucifer, she went and prepared the mind of Adam for her experience, and after Lucifer has created the sex organ 'PENIS' on Adam, it was Eve who taught Adam how to have sexual intercourse, and in that process, she became the leader, and because Lucifer is the god of this world, and the Bible was written when he became god of this world, he gave marriage leadership to Eve. This only happens in the western world, not in Africa.

Before Eve sinned, she had only the spirit of the I AM that would not have experience death, and after Adam and Eve might have created the angels for the kingdom, Eve could have gone back into Adam to become one being, 'Elohim' to become the leader or choir master for the created angels to replace the one third of the angels that rebelled with Lucifer, and the disrupted first heaven be restored for the whole heavenly realm.

As soon as A dam lost the divine method of sowing by the 'word', and replaced it with the sowing by the 'SPERM' the system prepares the female children in the womb better than the male children, and the result is that most female children do better than male children in early maturity, while male children are struggling as they go through teenage life to adulthood.

Although males are trying to empower themselves by magical systems, female witches are in control of the world of witchcraft, and it is important to know that the power of witchcraft control this world owned by Lucifer-god and goddess. This sinful world was built by sinful Adamic generations, and it is the kingdom of god and goddess, and has no connection with Jesus, the revealed I AM in the kingdom of heaven. When Jesus came, HE said, my kingdom is not of this world (John 18:36).

As soon as Lucifer remade Adam and Eve in his own image, the 'MAN-spirit' of the I AM left and the spirit of Lucifer-Satan entered Adam and Eve, and that became the human soul that everyone is born with. The presence of human soul means that everyone is the son or daughter of Lucifer and every person is a sinful being. Human soul is 'SIN' that Paul records in Rom 7 and the soul is the agent of sinful acts in human as recorded in Gal 5:19-21.

This is the foundation of human problems, but people's lack of knowing the truth, allow them to connect with god, the same god who is the cause of all human problems. Human beings are still in this world because most people do not know that they have to disconnect from the god of this world and connect to Jesus, the I AM to belong to the above.

The divine 'WORD' that Adam and Eve lost, was restored through the conception of Jesus when angel Gabriel spoke the 'WORD' to Mary and Mary received it and was pregnant without a man's sperm (Luke 1:31). Jesus taught his disciples the truth and the lost 'WORD' and after he has gone back to heaven, he sent his Holy Spirit to Peter and those who listened to him preach (Acts 2:1-). It was there that the Holy Spirit 'restored' the 'word' and language, and everyone heard one another irrespective of one's ethnic, tribe, race, culture, religion, and nation. It was from there that Peter and other disciples of Jesus were hated by the Jews and all of them were killed.

It was from there that the revealed and restored 'WORD' was hidden from human understanding because the real Jesus as an African was hidden and the records about him were distorted to represent fake Jesus Christ. This is why people speak in tongue with no understanding.

This will be restored immediately people disconnect from god and fake Jesus Christ, a white European Savior and connect with Jesus, the I AM, an African the Creator. The hidden word in the tongue was the original African language.

The change of the divine method of creation did a lot of damage to humanity. After the creation of 'illegal sex organs on Adam and Eve' by Lucifer for procreation through human SPERM, instead of sowing by the 'word' spiritually, sexual intercourse became an act of evil, and restored what Lucifer told Eve that she 'will know good and evil (Gen 3:5). This is why we have sexual immorality, sexual crimes and sexual abuse around the world.

For example, one in every four woman in Sweden is a victim of rape, more than 25,000 cases of child abuse, including sexual assault are reported each year in Pakistan, more than 3000 cases of child rape and assault are reported yearly in South Africa, around 3200 cases of child abuse are reported every year in Bangladesh, around 7500 cases of child abuses were reported in India in 2011, around 11000 child abuse cases are reported yearly in Russia, in the United Kingdom, one in every 200 adults are a pedophile and more than 16000 cases of child abuse cases were recorded in England in 2012, annually more than 18000 of child abused cases emerge in Afghanistan, the United State deals with almost 20000 child abuse cases annually and Australia has the highest rate of child abuse close to 50000 cases each year. (1)

Incest was the first form of institutional abuse in the United States and it remains by far the most widespread. One in three-to four girls, and one in five to seven boys are sexually abused before they turn 18, and the overwhelming incidence of which, happens in the family. This deception by Lucifer-god affects the religious institutions.

See how clergy abuse shook Catholics to the core, causing internal division within the religious organization. Incest is a very destructive psychic and physical trauma that had demonetized and distorted the identity and social patterns of the victims.

It is very clear now that when Adam and Eve were created before they sinned, they were in the kingdom that I AM built for them with gold, diamond and precious stones as the duplicate of the heavenly realm, and it did not have vegetation, trees and all the objects that we see on land today until they sinned and were driven out to build their own physical world that we live in today. I am saying this with the reason to make a point.

The remaking of Adam and Eve in the image of Lucifer, the tempter, who became the god of this world, has turned Eve into what the Bible called 'Garden of Eden' and Adam into the 'Sower' into the garden. Now men are the sex slave worker who sow 'SPERM' into the women-garden, by the snake-PENIS, through the tunnel-VAGINA into the garden-womb, all physical and natural, instead of the 'word' invisible and spiritual. Whether you have a soul or both soul and spirit, they are locked into the body as Lucifer promised because when he sinned, he was locked into the body of a 'beast' and uses his spirit-satan to rule the world. This shows that no one is free until after death. After death, the human soul-ghosts walks around in the supernatural realm still in this world and human beings cannot see them because the souls are in the body-prison that blinds them. Religions help human beings to function in the physical, and after death, they found out that they served Lucifer-god of this world that has no connection with Jesus and the heavenly realm, no one goes to heaven as male and female, it will happen when two become one as an angel since there is no marriage in heaven, and the created sexual evil does not exit in heaven.

The entire Old Testament must be rejected except the words of comfort by Jesus, because it presents the old history of the fight between Lucifer-god-Satan and Eve-goddess-devil. The scripture in John 21:25 says that Jesus did so many things that if they were to be written, the whole world will not contain such books. This shows that most of the things that Jesus did are not the Bible.

This means that the little portion in the Bible had been distorted and corrupted to represent the fake 'Jesus' called Christ, and must be rewritten through the divine revelation of the Holy Spirit, in order to present the real Jesus as the revealed I AM who came as the 'Mediator', 'Redeemer' and 'Savior' to save humanity and restore the first level of heavenly realm, disrupted by Lucifer, the rebel and fallen angel who has deceived the world for millions of years.

Religious organizations are also deceptive because they follow the Lucifer-god who runs this world, because people mistakenly took him as the creator and they worship him as the almighty.

Lucifer the archangel and the choir master wanted to overthrow the I AM and take the thrown to be worshipped and he was kicked out. He succeeded in achieving his desire when he remade Adam and Eve in his own image, humans had been procreated with the soul from Lucifer-god, and now millions of people are worshipping Lucifer as god in the religious gatherings.

The new 'MAN' that is the human 'soul' operates in human by the religious laws created bu Lucifer-god. As soon as Adam and Eve received the new 'MAN' as the human soul from Lucifer-god, the word 'LOVE' change from its divine nature of spiritual function to the fleshly nature of lust and immorality because of the evil sexual intercourse created by Lucifer-god that first destroyed the respect and angelic love relationship between Adam and Eve.

The real love had moved from the heart to the mind in which the eyes lust after anything it sees and transfers to the sex organs, that results in sexual intercourse. Real love is in the heart, and individual sees through the eyes of the heart. The love of the heart produces the power called 'AFFECTION' and this energy first wants holy angelic relationship and individual spouse does not have the holy affection to project to one another.

I strongly believe that Lucifer had a conversation with Eve, in which Eve told him the rules of the kingdom and her position as the helper to Adam. That had opened an opportunity for Lucifer to convince Eve to rebel against the 'MAN' Adam, to become the head and not the helper.

He put Eve's frame of mind in the same thought - process that he had to overthrow the I AM, and he was expelled from the kingdom of heaven. Eve accepted the idea of becoming a leader of the kingdom and yielded herself to Lucifer's plan to change her and her godhead Adam. This is where the conflict between male and female, man and woman, husband and wife started, just because the 'SEXUAL IDENTITY' was created by Lucifer and he is the god-Satan-god of this world till this day. The reign of Eve as the goddess of this world, after she had listened to Lucifer and succeeded to bring down Adam, is discussed in separate chapters.

Here she did destroy the leadership of Adam –MAN and upheld the leadership for Eve as the goddess. The result of her action put the entire African race under Lucifer as slave. What Africans are going through now as racism, oppression, domination and exploitation, are the results of what was introduced to them from the beginning of creation by Lucifer's deception.

Eve-devil-goddess continue to punish Africans till this day for not following her, but follow Lucifer-Satan-god as their almighty god. Africans do not see and know that all the development-religions, politics, economy, education and technology are done by Lucifer-Satan-god for his Luciferian racial groups only, and because Africans are not following her, the physical development of African world was locked into the world of witchcraft by Lucifer-Satan-god, since the first created African man Adam was dethroned.

Adam-god-Africa

My discussions have already shown that Adam was the created being, and the title 'god' was given to him by his Creator, the I AM. The Bible does not explain it because it was written from the time Lucifer became god. Adam and his generations built this world that we live in now, on top of the earth that covers the lost first level of kingdom of heaven built with gold, diamond and precious stones (Fig1).

This means that the whole Adamic world was one globe called Africa. A place where Adam and Eve were created as human beings.

I am presenting these revelations that the holy spirit gave me in order to put an end to some scientific claims that Africans evolved from apes. Some scientists made a mistake to see African as the wellspring of human genetic diversity, and as the origin of modern human which envisions a wave of Homo Sapiens, migrated earlier from Africa and interbreed with local Homo Erectus populations in multiple regions of the globe (Wolpoff at all, 2000).

Charles Darwin was the first to state that all humans had in common ancestors who lived in Africa, after he has studied 'out of African Hypothesis' and behavior of African apes which was displayed at the London zoo. Moreover, other researchers supported the hypothesis with the claim that African apes have a close evolutionary relationship with human (Robinson, 2010).

All these studies promote evolution as the efforts to prove that Africans evolved from chimpanzee, gorilla, monkey. This mistake is lack of knowing that the Adam and Eve were created as human beings, and that they are different from the angels who were deceived by Lucifer to rebel against 'MAN' and 'Adam-god' and were locked into the body as lower beings called animals as punishment.

Another mistake is that they do not know that two racial group came out of the woman Eve.

The first was: Lucifer and Eve' that gave birth to Cain, and that established Cainite-Caucasian race as Luciferian lineage.

The second was Adam and Eve, and that gave birth to Seth, and that established the Adamic-Canaanite-African lineage.

After intermarriage between the two group, the mixed racial group emerged as the third in the African globe, called the world (Mbosowo, 2012).

This shows that Adam as the first god, was an African, and as the first god, was an African before Lucifer deceived him and become the god if this world till this day.

Through the study of Genetic Reconstruction Jones and Savino (2007) found that all people alive today have inherited the mitochondria and was supported by Cann and Rhetal (1987) with further discovery that all the people living.

Today came from a woman who lived in Africa about 160,000, who was Eve. All the men living today have inherited their Y chromosomes from a man who lived 40,000-50,000 years in Africa, and has been named Y-chromosomal Adam.

These genetic reconstruction studies did a good job to identify African as the center of the origin of human beings, and as a confirmation that Africa was/is the place where the first family of Adam and Eve, that the Bible never mentioned. It will be wrong for some science students to mix up the animal lineage with the human lineage in order to label Africans as humans who evolved from animals.

This is racism that has refused to die out of humanity. We should give credit to the genuine and factual scientific studies that discredit the corrupted biblical records. Most people reject the scientific fact that the planet earth is 4.6 billion years and accept the biblical record that the earth is 2500 years old, because of religious conflict between facts and faith.

I am going to tell you what you have not known. The age of the earth as 4.6 billions years included the detail of the rule and works of Adam and Eve, as god and goddess, before Lucifer deceived them and took over as the god of this world. The billions of years that Adam and Eve ruled give account to the existence of Africa and the generations of African race before it was interrupted by Lucifer, the fallen angel.

The biblical record began with Lucifer, the fallen angel and the one who deceived Adam and Eve and because the god of Adam's world. The writers of the Bible, who were chosen by Lucifer-god, started the writing with the god who choose them as their own, and they hid the facts about that Adam's ruling for billions of years and the foundation of racism, that resulted in the destruction of the African generations by the Noah's flood (Mbosowo, 2010).

The Bible says that the earth is 1700 years old and scientific research records that the earth is 4.6 billions years old. This shows that Adam-god ruled for 3 billions years, Eve-goddess ruled for 1.5 billion years. The war between Lucifer-Satan-god and Eve-goddess-devil for change of leadership under Lucifer-Satan-god through religions took place for 99 million years. Lucifer recreated the earth ruled by the goddess with the light of the moon and put his light of the sun and ruled the earth for 998,000 years.

This shows that it took 1,700 years to put religions together that finally restored Lucifer as the one god of this world till this day.

Migration out of Africa:

Some scientists think that the people in Africa migrated out of Africa into other parts of the world. all these scientific studies show that the whole earth was one globe called Africa, that was built by Adam and Eve, as the first human family and their generations. After the golden kingdom was taken away from them because of sin. It then shows that the I AM, the Supreme Creator, who created Adam as the first god in African was /is an African.

The questions are: if there was only globe for Adam and Eve, how did we have different racial groups and nations divided by oceans, and how did the people cross the oceans from Africa to live in those nations?

If the I AM created Adam and Eve as the first African family, where did other racial groups come from?

The answer is, the Great I AM created a kingdom made of gold, diamond, silver and precious stones for Adam as the god of the kingdom, in order for him to create gods and angels on the first level of the kingdom of heaven that was messed up and was cut off from the second and third sections of the heaven because of lucifer's rebellion, but Adam made a mistake and listened to Eve and Lucifer, and the kingdom was taken away. Adam was asked to build his own world. Adam built this present world but lost it to Lucifer who became the god of this world.

It was sexual relationship that lucifer had with Eve that brought in another racial group through 'Cain' and the intermarriage between Adamic an Luciferian groups that created other racial groups and all of them live in the African world (Mbosowo, 2012).

Lucifer became god and the creator of another racial group through sexual union with Eve in the person called 'CAIN'. The division of the one globe into different continents, based on culture, language, religion and racial groups, might have happened about a few million years ago.

It was done mainly by the Luciferian racial group that wanted to separate themselves from the African. They dug the ground of about a mile to two mile wide, and as soon as they got to the top or surface of the land, they opened up for water from the ocean to run through the pathway, and that separated certain sections of the whole globe, to become different continent according to culture, language and skin color. Africans who were trapped in each of these different groups as the owners of the land were killed and those different lands were renamed to represent the different groups as the owners of the land called 'continents, with different countries'.

I strongly believe in this perspective for one reason. On February 13th, 2016, the holy spirit ministered to me that the colonial masters will separate North and South Africa from the continent of Africa. I asked why and I was told that those are the two important location of wealth and the mind of the citizens there had already been destroyed.

I was told that they have already gone far in making highways underground, and as soon as they get to the top of the land, they will direct water from the oceans to flow through and separate North and South Africa into two different countries for the Arabs in the North and the Dutch Jews and Europeans in the South.

This is scary because the separated North and South African will be given new names, and mineral wealth in those lands will be theirs, and Africans there will work for them as slaves, and after some time, African there will be killed.

This may not bother a lot of Africans because African mind has been buried in the religious grave, and they put their mind into religions and have become heavenly inclined and earthly useless. I am not criticizing the scientific studies, but I want to put an end to racism that claims that Africans evolved from apes. All that had been done in order to reduce Africans to the level of animal and be able to control their mind to accept their position as slaves and the wounded sheep who want to go to heaven.

The missing link:

The Bible only refers to Adam as the one who listened to his wife and ate the forbidden fruit and surrendered humanity to the tempter.

What is lacking in the Bible is the record of millions of years that Adam himself as god ruled the kingdom given to him by his Creator, the I AM, before Lucifer, the fallen angel-Satan, was able to corrupt the angels who served Adam to rebel against Adam, Adam became lonely (Gen 2:18). It was the entire position of Adam as god who ruled for millions of years that the Bible writers shifted to Lucifer who deceived Adam and Eve and became God, and Lucifer's spirit-Satan, was brought in as the one who tempted Adam through Eve (Gen 3:15).

The records show that the original contents of the Bible were copied from the ancient records of the Egyptians, Canaanites and Mesopotamians. All these places are African lands, meaning the original records were all about Africans and their lands. This then means that in the process of translation into Greek, Latin, Hebrew and then English, followed by different cultures, religions and languages, and those translations destroyed all the words and information associated with Africa in the original ancient record they copied from, and the present scriptures show the religious believes systems of those racial groups who stole from the African ancient records, and then buried or destroyed the ancient records that kept African race out of existence. They then developed religions that defined what they stole from Africa as evil, but they practice it in secret as god.

The burial of every good work by Adam as god and the turning of Adam into the man who brought curse on the ground (Gen3:17), were done by the Bible writers because Adam, being the first created being, was an African. Adam was stupid to listen to his wife Eve and fell to Lucifer's temptation, and lost the spirit of I AM, and received another 'MAN=SPIRIT' from Lucifer, which is the human 'SOUL' that represents 'Satan' lucifer's spirit. The scripture in Eph 2:2 explains 'the prince of the power of the air the spirit that now works in the children of disobedience'. This scripture has two faces, first it shows that Lucifer-Satan is the prince of the power of the air, meaning Lucifer's spirit 'Satan' is the prince in the kingdom of the air, lucifer's heaven in this universe for humans who follow him. Second face 'the spirit that now works in the children of disobedience' means that it was/is the same spirit that was given to Adam by Lucifer during temptation, which is the same one in human beings called the 'SOUL'. Human soul is the agent of sin. Paul confirmed this in (Gal 5:19-21) "the works of the flesh (soul) are adultery, fornication, lewdness, idolatry, witchcraft, hatred, contentions, jealousy, outburst of wrath, selfish ambition, dissension, envy, murders, drunkenness, revelries and the like'.

These characteristics of human soul represent the nature and characteristics of Lucifer-Satan in man, and by a simple command from Satan, human beings with these evil characteristics will turn against themselves and different kinds of problems that occur in the world today.

Adam sinned and the entire Adamic-African race was subject to physical and spiritual slavery under Luciferian –Cainite-Caucasian groups (Mbosowo, 2015). The creation continues to groan till this day because when Jesus came as the revealed I AM and as African, to restore the 'Spirit of the I AM', the truth was either destroyed or hidden, and fake JESUS was introduced through different religions that could/cannot solve the problems of humanity till this day (Mbosowo, 2015). It was here that Africans rejected Jesus because they were threatened by the slave masters.

The entire sinful world built by Adam and his generations, is now run by cultural, racial, religious and national gods, under the leadership of Lucifer-Satan who deceived Adam and became the god of this world. That happened after he was able to use different religions to eliminate the reign of Eve, the goddess who ruled the Adamic world for millions of years after Adam had died.

The Bible does not tell people that after Adam, the first created god, had lost the kingdom created for him by the I AM, and Adam was asked to build his own world, and he did, not by the 'word' but by both 'labor and lies' and that corrupted the 'word' to become the'world', and the Adamic world was run by goddesses and gods for millions of years until a man called Moses came into the scene, and he was the one who received by the spoken 'Word' the real and true name of the Creator as I AM (ex 3:14-15) and after too much suffering in the Adamic world, the I AM, the Creator revealed himself in the world to confirm the voice that spoke to Moses in the person of Jesus (Jh 8:58). Jesus, the revealed I AM came as the Mediator, Redeemer and Savior, to stop the fights, wars between Lucifer=Satan-god and Eve-devil-goddess, in order to help humanity and restore human beings back to the I AM, the Creator who created Adam, but he fell into the hands of Lucifer, the rebel, the fallen angel.

Brothers and sisters, let us clean up our minds of all the lies and receive the truth to be saves. I want to tell Africans that your great grand- fathers rejected Jesus who came to save them because they were afraid of the slave masters. Jesus came as the I AM (John 8:58), as an African, from the Great I AM, the Creator, an African, who created Adam and Eve, the first created beings, as the fist African family.

It is very sad that after billions of years, the people called Africans are still afraid of the slave masters, and cannot see the truth and disconnect from the god of this world, and connect with Jesus, as their own, not a Jew, so that African race can rise from the bottom of the universe.

The scripture says that 'and He died for all, that those who live should no longer live for themselves but for him who died for them and was raised again (2cor5"15).

Here Jesus came and died for the Africans who were enslaved by the Caucasians for millions of years. He rose from the death to set the slaves free, but Africans do not benefit from the resurrection of Jesus, because they rejected Jesus for fear of slave masters, and for that reason, Africans are still in the religious grave and are still suffering from spiritual slavery.

On July 3rd 2019, I had a revelation while in shower between 10 and 11 am. As I was about to get out, the holy spirit told me that only generational curse keeping the entire African race at the bottom of the universe is that their great grand- parents rejected Jesus, and after millions of years Africans are still blind to the truth. This curse will be removed immediately Africans reject the fake Jesus and accept Jesus, the I AM, as an African who came to save them.

CHAPTER FIVE

Eve-Devil-Goddess Ruled The World

The concept Devil

Webster's New World College Dictionary, defines the world 'Devil' as chief evil spirit, a supernatural being subordinate to, and the foe of god and tempter of human beings.

In I Peter 5:8:the scripture sees the devil as the enemy of human beings. This means that the devil wages wars, and creates problems for humanity.

Christianity, Judaism and Islam define the devil as the most powerful evil spirit and the ruler of hell. The first mistake most people made was to define the devil as 'HE'.

In this book, I define the 'Devil' as the spirit of Eve that is against Satan, the spirit of Lucifer. Religions like Christianity, Judaism, and Islam define the devil as a powerful spirit, and regard the devil as 'HE', and as the ruler of hell.

Western cultures defines devil as either Lucifer or devil. This is not right. Lucifer and Devil are two different beings as Lucifer-Satan-god and Eve-devil-goddess. Some writers define the devil as the leader of fallen angels, because they regard Lucifer as the devil, and so many portions of the Bible regard Lucifer as the devil.

The devil that is Eve's spirit, is not the leader of the fallen angels. Eve was not created until after thousands of years that Lucifer and one third of the angels were buried under the body of water, that was later made dry land, and the kingdom was built for 'MAN' then Adam and Eve came into being. It is difficult to destroy the devil because the religious systems are operated by the influence of the devil that uses the power of witchcraft as weapon of war against humanity. The devil is the spirit of Eve, and it is one being, but many religions use it wrongly to mean Satan.

The devil that is the spirit of Eve is fighting Satan, the spirit of Lucifer who is the god of this world.

I advise people to take note of this; lucifer, the rebel who was driven out of heaven, is defined as 'light leader' in Latin and in Hebrew, as 'son of dawn or morning star'. These definitions mean that when he was driven out of heaven into the Adam's world, he deceived Eve and then Adam-god of the kingdom, and became the god of Adam's world. as the god of this world, he has the government of the day, because of his nature of 'morning star' and light bearer.

Devil, the spirit of Eve is defined as 'evil' and with her power of witchcraft, she had the government of the night. This is where the confusion between 'Satan; to 'devil' came into existence. People have mistakenly regarded the 'god', a title given to Adam as the god of the kingdom, as the supreme creator, when Lucifer deceived Adam and became god of Adam's world, and used his spirit 'Satan' to rule the world, people then saw the 'devil' as 'Satan' against god.

I have observed that only the presence of Satan and his activities dominate the entire Bible, and anything about the 'devil' will refer one to Satan. This will be discussed in detail in a separate chapter. This shows that Lucifer who became god, has used his spirit 'Satan' to knock out Eve and allowed her to rule the night.

The scripture defines Lucifer's rebellious behaviors as the power of witchcraft (1Sam.15:23). This means that it is the witchcraft power, used in the present world, because it is Lucifer who is the bearer of that power that is the god of this world. It means that both Lucifer-god and Eve-goddess are using the power of witchcraft to rule the world in the day and the night.

Most Christians are made to believe that the 'devil' was once a mighty angel who was at God's presence until he rebelled. This is related to Lucifer because he rebelled against the I AM, the Creator, and took thousand of years before the kingdom of the land was created. Adam was created, and the title god was given to him, in which the Bible does not explain (Mbosowo, 2007).

For this reason, the devil was not Lucifer, rather it was Eve, who was with Adam as her god and her husband. This confusion existed because the Bible does not explain the thousands of years that Adam ruled the kingdom as god until the fallen angel Lucifer-Satan was able to corrupt all the angels under Adam and he became lonely (Gen. 2:18), and that made the I AM to change from creation to procreation, where Eve was made for Adam.

While Lucifer uses his spirit 'Satan' to rule the world as god, after he has convinced Eve to stand with him to overthrow Adam, Eve then uses her spirit devil to enslave human beings particularly males with her power of witchcraft, and Lucifer who transformed himself into the angel of light (2Ccor 11:14-15), and became the prince of this world (John 14:30), the god of this world (2Cor 4:4), the prince of the air (Eph 2:2), had been seen by many religions as the 'morning star' and he had the opportunity to rule as god of the universe.

In the Bible, Lucifer is god and he uses his spirit 'Satan' to deceive human beings, that Satan is the enemy of god.

The Judgment day:

The I AM, the Supreme Creator created only life and he has no part in the concept of 'death', for this reason, the I AM will not judge his spirits that are with him as his divine children or angels. The I AM did not create evil and he will not have a judgment day. This judgment day is for human souls created by Lucifer-god, based on the religious laws that he made for the human souls to keep. The human soul was created during deception. Adam was deceived by Lucifer and he lost the spirit of the I AM and received the spirit of Lucifer that became the human soul, and the human soul is the agent of evil in human beings. The judgment is for the evil acts done by the human soul (Gal5:19-21). It is important to know that any scripture in the Bible that refers to god is talking about Lucifer who deceived Adam, overthrew him as god the kingdom and became the god of this world till this day. Lucifer took over the world built by Adam after he was driven out of the kingdom built for him by the I AM, a place the Bible calls the garden of Eden, and now Lucifer –god is building his kingdom called the 'kingdom of god'. It is the god of this world that will judge the souls of humans beings who did not keep the religious laws created by god of this world and very important, the kingdom of god has nothing to do with the kingdom of heaven where Jesus dwells.

The Bible writers started their story with 'god' who was Lucifer and they either hid or destroyed all the records of what Adam did as an African, in order to present only the work of Lucifer, for the Caucasian racial groups to rule over the African race.

The I AM who created Adam, revealed himself in Jesus (John 8:58) as the Savior for the enslaved Africans, but after HE has completed his work and went back to heaven, Lucifer-god directed the Caucasian racial groups to create religions that controlled African mind and got it buried in the religious grace till this day, and all the records of the works of Jesus were distorted and corrupted and another Jesus was introduced to become the son of god Lucifer (Mbosowo, 2015).

This show that all the people who claim to follow this god and the fake Jesus are the children of Satan (John 8:44).

Why is it so difficult to understand the command that the I AM gave to Moses that as from that moment, his name was I AM and must go for generations (Ex3"14-15). This means that I AM, the Creator rejected the name that was/is Lucifer title. He is the god that rules the entire universe.

The duties of the devil:

The scripture says that Lucifer's rebellion is the same as witchcraft. Lucifer first met Eve and convinced her to rebel against her master and god, Adam, and she lost her divine spirit and received from Lucifer the power of witchcraft.

Witchcraft was the first religion that pays full attention to Eve, who became the goddess of this world after Adam was defeated and put out and she used her spirit 'devil' to run the religious organization called witchcraft. Let us see the activities of the devil in the Bible.

Evidence of witchcraft as the devil's work in the Bible:

The presentation of the presence of Satan devil and witchcraft in the Bible show the work of Lucifer-Satan and Eve-devil as they use the power of witchcraft to rule humanity on earth.

In I Sam 28:7 the scripture says:

Then Saul said to his servants, find me a woman, who is a medium that I may go to her and inquire of her and his servants said to him' in fact, there is a woman, who is a medium at En Dor. (NKJV)

Here Saul went to the representative of the goddess-Eve, the devil for help.

In 2 Chro33:6: the scripture says:

After King Manasseh has built alters to worship the hosts of heaven and serve them, also he causes his sons to pass through the fire in the Valley of the son of Hinnom, he practiced soothsaying used witchcraft and sorcery and consulted mediums and spiritists. He did much evil I the sigh of the Lord to provoke HIM to anger (NKJV)

Here King Manasseh operated by the power of witchcraft, the power of goddess, while serving god-lucifer-Satan, and the writer's suggested that such confrontation would make god angry.

In 2 Kings 9:22: the scripture says:

Now it happened, when Joram saw Jehu, that he said 'is it peace Jehu?' so he answered 'what peace, as long as the harlotries of your mother and her witchcraft are so many' (NKJV). Here King Ahab was on the side of Lucifer-god but his wife Jezebel was the representative of Eve-goddess, the devil, and she overpowered the king. This is the war between Lucifer-god-Satan and Eve-goddess-devil.

In Ex: 22:18, the scripture says:

Thou shalt not suffer a witch to live (KJV).

HERE Lucifer who deceived Adam and became the god of this world, decided to allow those who followed him as their god, to kill women who practiced witchcraft and followed Eve, the goddess. They disconnected from IAM, the true Creator and are fighting between two of them.

In 2Cor 11:13-14,Paul saw how false apostles, deceitful workers transformed themselves into apostles of Christ. Satan himself transforms himself into an angel of light. Paul found out that members if the church were ministers of Satan. This means that after Lucifer-Satan had transformed himself into an angel of light, human beings followed him as god, not knowing that they are serving him as Lucifer-Satan-god.

In I Tim 2:1-12, Paul presents the conflict between Lucifer-Satan-god and Eve-devil-goddess. The war was that women were silenced in the church in order to exclude the presence of goddess. That was the way to stop women from using the power of witchcraft to control and manipulate men for their Eve-goddess-devil.

The concept 'devil' has been wrongly defined because human beings with the soul that came from Lucifer during the deception, are on the side of Lucifer –Satan-god, particularly males, and Eve-goddess-devil fights back. In the mainstream Judaism, the concept of devil is not recorded, meaning the word devil does not exist as recorded in Christianity, but the word 'Satan' is mentioned in the Old Testament books of Zechariah (3:1-3) and Job (1-11). In the mainstream Christianity, the devil is referred to as Satan. This is wrong. The words devil and Satan are different and they refer to two different beings as opponents. In the Bible, the scripture identifies the devil with dragon and the 'old serpent' in Rev 12:9, and also identified devil with Satan and as 'the prince of this world" (John 12:31; 14:30) and the 'spirit that now worked in the children of disobedience Eph 2:2), and the god of this world (2cor 4:4). These explanations are the mixture of two different beings together as one. This book gives the correct explanations of these two forces as different beings as separate and as opponents.

In Islam, the concept devil is referred to as Iblis, and sometimes called shaytan, that was created by god out of fire, and was among the angels whom god ordered to bow down to Adam after his creation.

People follow god and pray to him. Sometimes he answers, sometimes he does not answer. The main reason god tries to answer people's prayers and requests is to keep them on his side against Eve-goddess-devil, that has been stigmatized as evil, and through religions, everyone that follows god, prays against the devil, and this has created a boundary between god and goddess, and has resulted in the spiritual and physical wars that had affected humanity for millions of years. These are the wars between the two opposing beings Lucifer-Satan-god and Eve-goddess-devil, that religious organizations do not know about.

Eve-devil-goddess ruled the world:

Adam's sin of breaking the divine instructions given to him by the I AM, his creator, was serious because the I AM created him first and gave him instructions and directions on how to restore the disrupted first level of the kingdom of heaven by Lucifer.

It was after Lucifer has corrupted the angels that served Adam that he became lonely, just because all the angels that listened to Lucifer and rebelled against Adam were all locked into the body of lower beings as animals and their ability to communicate with Adam was taken away, and Adam then became lonely.

It was then that the I AM removed the female part in Adam-Elo and made a woman for Adam, and Adam was the one who instructed the woman-Eve on the rules and regulations on how to run the kingdom. This means that when Eve came with an idea contrary to what the IAM gave him, it was his responsibility to reject it and throw Eve out of the kingdom, and she alone could have been locked into the body of an animal. He did not, and he lost the nature, the spirit of I AM and the goddess to Lucifer, while Eve became the goddess of the world that he built with his generations, and the Bible does not talk about.

Is it ignorance or deceptive cover up?

When Adam yielded to Eve's new idea and later submitted to Lucifer's idea, the original plan of procreation changed. Adam was driven out of the kingdom, and he built his own world that we live in now, and after Lucifer was locked into the body of the beast and his ability to communicate with other beings, Eve was ready to rule the world after Adam had lost his leadership and Lucifer was in prison for thousands or a million years, according to the agreement she made with Lucifer as recorded in Gen 3:5

For god knows that in the day you eat of it, your eyes will be opened and you will be like god, knowing good and evil (NKJV).

I want everyone to know that the god mentioned in this scripture refers to Adam, the god of the kingdom, who received all the instructions from the I AM, his Creator. It was that deception that convinced Eve to listen to Lucifer in order to be like her god master Adam. It was now that Eve had the opportunity to rule the world. a place that Adam built with 'labor' not 'word' now the 'world'.

I want to look at many sources that offer some information where different racial groups worshipped and are still worshipping her today. If Eve, the goddess ruled the world for thousands or millions of years, I strongly believe that her world was empowered by the light of the moon, in which was cut off by Lucifer after he was released from prison and gain his ability to speak and used his spirit-Satan to rule.

The moon as the goddess throne in the solar system:

Many researcher had been done on the 'moon' to explain its formation, starting with its existence of 4.6 billion years, with 150 mile-radius, with the measurement of 1390 mile diameter, and with the presence of water dust, seasons that make a complete orbit around the earth, with distance between the Moon and the Earth at 252,700 miles, and the Moon's orbit is subtly perturbed by the Sun and Earth, in interacting ways, showing that both the moon and the sun are considered planet-satellite system because both of them have the same effect on earth, also the astrometry in Babylon, India, China, have studied the luna eclipses, elongation and solar cycles of the moon, and other nations, including United States, Japan, China, have explored the moon's internal structure. Russia and United States explored the outer space and theorized that the moon and all outer space formed the 'province of all mankind' (2).

These findings mean that the moon was the kingdom and the throne of the goddess where human souls dwell after death. If the ghosts of the dead were accepted into the kingdom of the moon, it then means that the goddess was the ruler of the universe.

Eve was the first goddess who ruled this world after Adam had failed and later died, and used the light of the moon for the seasons of the world, and the rock samples from the moons dated as old as 4.6 billion years shows that the goddess has ruled the world for a long time, but all her works had never been credited to her.

The ancient records have shown the moon goddess as an important deity in different cultures around the world, and are purely feminine in nature.

All the goddess in different cultures were under the leadership of Eve, the mother goddess. In Greece, the goddess Aega was the beautiful moon deity, Andromeda is another Greek goddess that is linked to the stars, Artemis is the Greek goddess of the nature and birth, other Greek goddess include Bendis, who was the consort of the sun god Sabazius, Hekate, who carries a touch as the symbol of her great wisdom and Selen who is being worshipped by those they called pagans.

In Persia, Anahita, the river goddess, was also goddess of Venus, and her name means 'pure of immaculate one' who represented the cleansing and fertilizing flow of the cosmos. In Babylon, Anunit, the goddess of the moon for the battle, and after her association with the evenong star, she became known as Ishtar.

In Africa, Arawa, the luna goddess of suk and Pokot tribes in Kenya and Uganda, also Jezanna, the goddess of the moon and healing in Central Africa. In China, the goddess Chano-O lives in the moon and she is being celebrated to this day on full moon night of the 8th lunar month. A Buddhist goddess Iyotsna, was the goddess of compassion and healing. In Rome, Diana is the goddess of the moon, responsible for fertility and childbirth; Epona was the goddess of the night, dreams, magic, fertility and feminine power, Juna was the goddess of the new moon, marriage, pregnancy, and childbirth, and was worshiped by women.

Goddess Lucina was associated with light, both solar and lunar. She was christianized as St. Lucia, a saint still honored at Yule in many part of Europe. In Japan, goddess Izanami controlled the tides, fishing and all destructive sea phenomena. In Egypt, the goddess Sefkhet was the deity of time, the stars and the architecture.

Isis was the goddess and deity of the moon and goddess of the sun as well.

Some writers believe that there are moons in other planets as it is in the planet earth. This shows that the goddess ruled every planet that existed before the planet earth, and her influence is still in the previous planets that closed down because the truth was, either distorted, deleted or hidden. The moon is here in this planet earth and the goddess and goddesses are in every nation, culture religion as the power that fights gods who use the sun to rule the earth, and it will soon be closed down because the truth is not presented to the world, in order to set humanity free from the religious bondage and spiritual slavery. Let us reveal what is under this sinful and fake world, so that the truth will be restored for peace and harmony for humanity.

Goddess ruling and matriarchal status:

During the rule of the goddess, matriarchal was the order of the day, because the ancient societies worshipped the goddess and women were holding high status. Many researchers have presented valuable records of the worship of goddess, that gave women the high status and control of societies. (Klein, 1996) found that in the ancient society, women were the main sources of wealth, and that women were the owners of the house as well as the producers of food, shelter and security for the family, and that a man was dependent upon a woman economically. Stone (1976) presented very good information on the supreme status of goddess and high status of women before it was destroyed by the men.

In the ancient Egypt, the goddess held supremacy status, husbands stayed at home and weaved, while wives were out for the family wealth. In the family, women had the position for inheritance passed through the mother, rather than through the father (Stone, 1976), and the women's condition was high due to economic independence and all property went in the female line, and in every home, a woman was the mistress of the house and in control of herself and the place(Stone, 1976:37).

Women were free as late as the fourth century BC, in a form of marriage in which the wife chose the husband and could divorce him on payment of compensation (Stone, 1976 : 37). It was the daughters, not the sons who were the actual inheritors of the royal home (Murray, 1921).

For generations, people had been living in a land where women held a very high status and matrilineal descent system continued until it was interrupted by the male religious status.

In the ancient Ethiopia and Libya in 49 BC, all authority was vested in a woman. For example in Ethiopia, the women were the people who carried arms and were the one who practiced communal marriage and raised their children. In Libya, women were the authorities who discharged public duties, while men looked after domestic affairs and took care of the children at home as nannies. Women in Lybia were in armed forces that invaded other lands and worshipped Neith as their goddess whom they probably believed gave them power (Stone, 1976:34-35).

This matrilineal system of the goddess and higher position of daughters in the family is still practiced today by the tribe called 'Efik' in a town of Calabar, at the Cross River State in Nigeria, West Africa. The daughters inherit family property after the death of their parents, and if the sons live in houses built by the parents, they have to pay rents to their sisters, and also pay for any land the parents left behind if they want to build their houses on it. Here the women are still worshipping the goddess and maintain a specific day each year, they go in a boat and sacrifice to goddess in the sea.

In the ancient Greece, Gaia was refereed to as the mother goddess, and the mother earth who gave birth to the sea gods that became giants. The Greek legend of the goddess known as Hera, and women were of high standing, and were around holy places and allowed women to be in control of temples, in which they worshipped the goddess and were also in the state festivals of the goddess (Stone, 1976).

In the ancient India, the people worshipped the goddess and through the Aryan invaded the indigenous population, the people of India still retain the worship of goddess, it is also observed that the Great Mother is widely worshipped in India, and goddess Sarrasvati was honored in India as the one who invented the original alphabet.

In the ancient Canaan, some researchers discovered that before Canaan was invaded by foreigners, the Canaanites were worshipping the goddess Astarte as the head goddess that was identical with the Egyptian Hathor that was borrowed from Mesopotamia, as identified through the plagues as prehistory in the early bronze age (Albright, 1941). The idea was further supported that the Arstarte plague had existed right down to the 7th century BC (Kenyon, 1960). This shows that all other goddess were under her control. Archaeological records and artifacts reveal that the religion of the goddess as Ashtoreth, Arstarte, Asherah, Anath, Elat or Baalat still flourished in many of the great cities of Canaan.

Most writings about the Jews question whether god had a wife, and that made them to try to avoid the goddess reign on earth for millions of years. They are trying to avoid the truth that Adam, the first being created by the I AM was god and his wife Eve was the goddess who built this present world, after they had lost original kingdom that the I AM gave to them. Adam and Eve built this sinful world and they are the god and goddess of this world, while other gods and goddess are under them as cultural, racial, religious and national gods. As long as Adam and Eve were the first created Africans, all other local gods, religious and racial gods are under Adam and Eve, the Africans.

Eve ruled the world that Adam built with Lucifer's power of witchcraft. The word "witchcraft' came from the rebellious character of Lucifer when he rebelled against the I AM and he was expelled from the throne of I AM, and his behavior was defined as witchcraft (1Sam. 15:23).

Lucifer first met with Eve and made her rebel against Adam, the god of the kingdom, and the power of witchcraft was passed unto Adam. Adam and Eve lost the kingdom built for them by the I AM, and Adam used the power of witchcraft to build the world that we live in now.

Adam was the god of his world, but he lost it to Lucifer, who deceived him and became the god of the this world that he built, and after Lucifer was locked into the body of the beast and Adam lost his position, Eve became the goddess and ruled this world for thousands or millions of years, with the power of witchcraft, which became the belief system called religion in the world that was transformed from Lucifer to the African race, and from there it became the ancient African religion, because it was brought to Africans by the first African goddess. Because Adam and Eve sinned against their Creator, the I AM and lost the spirit of I AM, they disconnected from the I AM and connected to Lucifer, the deceiver who became their god and gave them the power of witchcraft that Eve used to govern the world after the death of Adam for thousands or millions of years.

From this perspective, witchcraft became the supernatural power that controlled Africa and the whole world since the whole globe belonged to the Adamic African race, and lucifer who brought the rebellious behavior defined as witchcraft (Isam15:23) is the god of this world (Eph.2:2 ; John 14 : 30).

The other non-African racial groups in the world evolved from Lucifer through his son Cain that Eve had for him during temptation and deception, and all human racial groups in the world are controlled by the power of witchcraft because Lucifer whose rebellious behavior was the manifestation of witchcraft is the god of this world till this day. This shows that Lucifer –god Satan and Eve-goddess-devil are the two forces that use the power of witchcraft to rule humanity in this world. The conflict between these two forces that brought problems to humanity will be discussed later.

This is an indication that Eve the goddess and the first African woman has authority as the mother nature over the nations of the world. This is why every race, culture, religion and nation has different types of goddesses that function according to the energies assigned to each goddess, under Eve the Goddess. The goddess created the moon as the kingdom of light that governed her world, and remained as the throne for the goddess, but after Lucifer was released from the prison of silence in the body of the beast he used his spirit 'Satan' and pushed the goddess to the kingdom of the sea and made the moon to function is a certain system called night, while he created the kingdom of the air and created the sun as the light for the world and called it day. This is where the Bible says that god created the earth in sex days (Gen 1:31).

For thousands or millions or years of goddess reign, there had been changes in the status of goddess under her, and this means that the goddesses we have in each nation today, represent the long line of leadership under Eve, the mother goddess. This is an indication that the present different cultures, belief systems and rules and regulations evolved from what Adam and Eve, the first African family and it concludes that the entire world and humanity owe its structure and processed to the African race.

The scripture says that the I AM commanded the water that covered the first level of the kingdom of heaven for thousands of years to gather together, and made one third of the portion to dry and he built a kingdom for his spirit beings called 'MAN'.

It was the duplicate of the kingdom realm made of gold, diamond and precious stones. Africa was that position where the kingdom was built and when Adam sinned, the kingdom was dislocated and turned upside down and covered with the element called sand and Adam was asked to build his world that we live in now, and human being have to suffer to make a living because of the curse put on the land because of Adam's sin.

Goddess evil acts against men

I define the concept to the word devil as the spirit of Eve, and the records refer to witches evil acts as the work of the devil. This shows that when Eve was the goddess and ruled the world for millions of years, she commissioned the goddess who worked for her as witches to punish men, in order to show that women were in control. During the reign of the goddess, witches did evil against men.

It is important to make this statement for clarification. The women's evil against men started with Eve's relationship with Lucifer. When Lucifer met with Eve, she opened up and told Lucifer all about her master Adam and all the rules in her home. Lucifer took advantage of it and convinced her that she would become the ruler-god of the kingdom and her master would be under her. She agreed and decided to work with him to overthrow Adam, and she became the goddess of Adam's world.

In Africa, witchcraft rules over the entire continent. The goddess and the queen of the government of the world of witchcraft has the power to destroy the male African children, particularly the first- born sons. Eve got the witchcraft power from Lucifer who was kicked out of the heaven by rebilling against the I AM, and his rebellious behavior was defined as witchcraft. Because Eve was the head of this devilish power, witchcraft has become the evil society dominated by women, and this has created the position for the wives and mothers who are witches to be the controllers of witchcraft in the families, and mothers have the upper hand to sacrifice or kill the male children with witchcraft and then pass the power to the female children.

Prominent researchers and writers observed that witches caused sterility in men. They turned the minds of men to inordinate love or hatred and struck them with lightening and killed some of them, they bewitched men with mere look without touching them and caused death. They also changed men into beast and took away men's sexual energy and caused diseases in their body. They controlled male organs in great numbers and put them in a bird's nest or shut them up in a box where they move themselves like living members and eat oath and corn. They caused barrenness in men and inflamed men toward women and rendered them impotent toward other women (Summers, 1971:99-168) such evil was further observed that witches hampered men's productive activities and made men's productive activities and make damage to those domestic pursuits in which they as women had the most training skill and control and that a witch caused a man's breast to swell like a woman's breast and burned the man's sexual organ (Karlsen, 1989:32,145).

The evil acts by the goddess against men show that Eve used the power of witchcraft to govern the world and the religion she used was witchcraft. Science, researchers and historical records show that the first world and the first creation which started in Africa, is the proof that the power of witchcraft was first used in Africa since Adam and Eve were the first family created by the I AM, the Creator. This means that after Adam and Eve were deceived and were disconnect from their Creator, the IAM, Africans and non-African racial groups were governed by Eve as the goddess before

Lucifer fought back to restore the male status through different religious beliefs apart from witchcraft.

It is very important to stress the ruling of Eve-goddess as a phenomenon that most human beings do not pay attention. In each month of the year, the moon shows up as the new moon, the full moon and the last quarter of the moon to prove that the goddess is still in operation in the world till this day. Even though Lucifer-god has pushed her to the night season, while he rules the world with the light of the sun in the day season.

This fight between Lucifer-god-sun and Eve-goddess-moon is hidden from human beings and such ignorance has made it so difficult to solve the religious-spiritual problems and natural disasters that had tortured the entire humanity for billions of years. I am calling upon the world to know the truth in order to find solution to the problem of humanity.

CHAPTER SIX

Lucifer, The Fallen Angel and His Activities

Lucifer was originally created the by IAM, the Supreme Creator, as one of the archangels and was made as the choir master and music director. He was decorated with precious stones. He occupied the first level of the kingdom of heaven with one third of angels and he had the duty of going up to the second heaven and at the center called firmament, he stood with his choir and offered praise and worship to the I AM, the Creator at the third heaven. He might have done that for billion of years, but the Bible does not talk about it. The Bible says that Lucifer rebelled against the I AM because of pride and I perceive that he had problem with jealousy, that pushed him to want to overthrow the IAM, and take his throne to be worshipped by the angels. He was expelled from the throne of IAM, and was restricted to the first level of the kingdom of heaven, and the place was covered with water for thousands of years and a boundary was created to prevent Lucifer from crossing over to the second heaven, and the holy spirit was appointed as the security agent on top of the body of the water, to prevent Lucifer and his angel from coming out of the body of water. After thousands of years, Lucifer was locked into the body of a beast, and all his angels that rebelled with him were locked into the body of the sea creature and mammals (Mbosowo, 2007). Lucifer is till in the body of the beast, but his rebellious behavior is what the scripture records as the spirit of witchcraft (1Sam.15:23), and this is the spirit that came into humanity through Lucifer and the whole world is controlled by the power of witchcraft. Lucifer deceived Adam and Eve, and they lost the divine nature and the spirit of IAM, as it happened to him Lucifer and Adam and Eve then received the nature of Lucifer and the spirit of witchcraft. Lucifer is still in the body of the beast till this day, and he uses his spirit-Satan to rule the world.

Satan: The word is defined as adversary, opponent. I define the concept Satan as the spirit, energy, power of Lucifer that works for him while he sits back as god of love, and human beings only know about the satanic activities toward humanity. (Ford, 2010:17-18) states that adversary is perceived as being the" light bringer and empowerment spirit in which the individuals model their initiation on, in which the mind is trained to think as a god or goddess, thus liberating the self from restrictive spirituality". The nature of Lucifer as explained by Ford shows that Lucifer was trying to separate himself from the God of the Bible. This is not true.

The Almighty Creator is the I AM (ex3:14-15) and HE created Adam as the first god of the kingdom he built for him and his partner Eve. Lucifer deceived Adam with the intention to become the god of that kingdom but the kingdom was dislocated, turned upside down and covered with the element called sand and Adam was asked to build his own kingdom. At the fall of Adam and Eve, they lost the spirit of IAM and received the spirit of Lucifer and became subject to him as their god. This shows that human soul is from Lucifer and that he will do all that he can to transform the human soul into a divine beings to be used for his kingdom.

This is the process of forming the kingdom of god that is different from the kingdom of heaven for the Great I AM and Jesus. This is why Luciferianism rebels against religious control and encourages individual to train his soul to acquire knowledge, self improvement wisdom and power and then become the transformed spiritual light. Lucifer is training human souls that are his representatives to become the gods for his kingdom, the kingdom of god on earth.

Luciferianism: Luciferianism is the official introduction of Lucifer by name and as god of this world, who is no longer hiding under the title god, in order to protect himself from the negative label of rebellion, 'satanic' and 'magical and occultist practices' so as to fit into the definition of his name as the morning star and the light bringer.

Ford (2010) defined Luciferianism as 'a modern' term of ideological, philosophical and magical attainment of applicable knowledge and inner power. The type of knowledge sought through study, initiation and the continual struggle for self improvement through spiritual rebellion against the social concept of god and religion, and views that Luciferianism is the ultimate spirituality as it focuses on the growth and expansion of the individual in a rational sense here and now with the broad range of spiritual exploration as well and further that Luciferianism encourages a strict adherence towards the self determined goals of the 'initiate' as well as the discipline of magical practices (vv16-17). This is Lucifer's behavior.

In in14:13 KJV calls Lucifer, son of the morning. NKJV calls him the son of the morning and other writers call him morning star, light bringing, and bringer of dawn; all these definitions do not portray the duty of Lucifer in the kingdom of heaven as the archangel, rather they show what Lucifer did after he has defeated Adam and made him disconnect from the IAM, and after Adam had lost his glory meant for the Adam-Seth-Ham-Canaan-African race, and was forced to build this world that became the kingdom of god for Lucifer the present god of this universe, all Adam did was turned to the luciferian (non African) race, through Cain's generations that wandered in the wilderness of darkness.

There is no day or night in the kingdom of heaven of the Great IAM. The kingdom of heaven is ruled and covered by light and Lucifer who was decorated with precious stone, appeared as light in the kingdom of heaven.

After he has sinned by rebelling against the IAM, he lost the divine nature and power as the angelic being and his rebellious behavior, nature, power and light became as power, nature and light of witchcraft, and his being changed into an opponent, adversary, enemy meaning 'Satan' which is the spirit being of Lucifer.

The scripture in is 14:3-4; ex1:14; lev17:7; 2cho11:15, rev18:2; was distorted and corrupted in order to hide the name Lucifer as the fallen angel and rather presented the king of Babylon as the fallen king, because of his evil acts against Israel, and that was the reason Babylon was destroyed. The Bible was written with this distorted information to hide the fall of Lucifer and his evil acts against the Africans who owned Babylon, after desribing Babylon as the home of demons and of evil spirits.

Lucifer who become the god of the Israelites saw the beauty and glory of Babylon (Is13:19) and promised to destroy the people and take the land (Is13:19-22). All the groups of people that were killed as recorded in the Bible were Africans, but Caucasian killed them and gave different names to those paces in order to hide the truth. Lucifer was the fallen angel and he turned himself into the angel of light (2Cor. 11:14), and people followed him as the light bearer. In Judaism, different people believed differently, in Is 14:12. the Hebrew believed in the fallen angel from heaven. In the medieval Judaism, the people rejected any belief in rebel or fallen angels but believed that evil is abstract (Bamberger, 2006). The Jewish exegesis of Is14:12-15, took a more humanistic approach by identifying the king of Babylon as Nebuchadnezer and this shows that the Jews hid the image of Lucifer because Lucifer made them the chosen people for himself, and then the Jews identified the king of Babylon as Nebuchadnezer in the place of Lucifer, just to make him their god, and then the god of the whole world.

That was the main reason why the IAM, the Supreme Creator revealed himself to Moses and commanded him to drop the title god and take up his real name IAM. The Jews followed up and hid the name IAM, and introduced other names as Yahweh, Jehovah, with the reason that the name IAM was too holy to mention.

Lucifer-god and his reign with the sun

After Lucifer had deceived Adam and Eve, he was locked up in the body of the beast for thousands of years. The meaning of his imprisonment is that he was unable to speak like other animals or sea mammals. During the thousands of years of imprisonment, Adam and Eve procreated and multiplied to fill the earth but the world was under the leadership of Eve, the goddess. After he was released and he was able to speak, he did not go straight to rule the Adams world because he made a deal with Eve that she would be like god after eating the forbidden fruit (Gen3:4-5).

Lucifer was and is still in the body if a beast, but he uses his spirit-Satan to rule the world. it looked like when Eve-goddess ruled with the light of the moon, the weather and atmosphere were cool and calm. Lucifer was able to push Eve-goddess into the kingdom of the sea and she became the queen of the kingdom of the sea.

The world must have been in darkness and Lucifer created his light for the earth called it "sun". The sun is in the kingdom of the air, where lucifer's spirit 'satan' makes his throne and it is called 'sky' and it gives light to the earth, in the system called day.

This is the general biblical belief that god is the one who created the world in six days (Gen1:31).

What the Bible talks about in Gen. 1 has to do with the process in which Lucifer was able to push Eve, the goddess into the kingdom of the sea, and he names it the sun and it gives light to create the season of day. In order for Lucifer to have a compromise with Eve-goddess, he allowed night in which the goddess continues to use the moon to rule the night. The day the goddess was pushed into the deep of the kingdom of the sea by Lucifer, the two glorious sisters 'harmony and beauty' left this world and they were replaced with noise, force, violence, crime, fake music, and falsehood. It was Adam and his generations that built this world and it was Eve who knew how to rule this world after Adam. The luciferian-Cainite racial groups who took over did not know what to do until they mixed with the Adam-African race, and stole the technological knowledge from Africa, and replaced it with religion to pray toward heaven as fools who lost their mind, and were defined as pagans and evil. Now Africans have the riches continent in the world but cannot tap it to feed the hungry population, rather pray to go to heaven but useless in the natural world. This is slave mentality and must change.

The three religions that Lucifer-god used is destroying the female goddess are Judaism, Islam and Christianity, in which they used after stealing. They created religions that define what they stole as evil. Laws and dogmas that promoted god and condemned goddess as evil and that resulted in the destruction of any image and shrines of the goddess. The early church fathers of the 3rd, 4th, and 5th century degraded women and argued that the female as a symbol of goddess was from satan and that there was a goddess in every woman that has to be crushed.

The founder of western theology, in his theological agreement, wrote that a woman is a temple built over a sewer, the gate-way to the devil and that women are the gate of hell (Roberts, 1924). Gimbutas (1989:319) wrote 'women were called disciples of satan and this period was one of the bloodiest in history. The witch hunts of the 15th to 18th centuries was the most satanic event of European history. The murder of women accused as witches escalated to more than eight million. The burned or hanged women were mostly country women who learned the love of the goddess from their grandmothers'.

Later, church fathers held degrading views of women and Martin Luther wrote that: 'if a woman grows weary and dies from childbearing, it does not mater, let her die bearing children, that is all she is here for'. At the grace Cathedral, before700 delegates fighting the ordinations of women, Episcopal Bishop C.L. Meyers commented that: 'a priest is a god symbol. God is masculine in both the Old and New Testament. Christ was a man, masculine. That was a divine choice'.

Later on when Catholicism became the dominant religion in Europe, goddess worship disappeared yet remnants of feminine divine can still be found in Virgin Mary, Sophia and female saints.

Although female religious figures disappeared almost completely with the protestant reformation, yet the presence of mother goddess and female goddesses role moel are present in all cultures and religions around the world. For example in Egypt are goddesses Anut, Bast, Bellona, Isis, Hathor, Menhit, Seshet, Sekhmet, the roman goddesses include Aurora, Diana, Arthemis, Juna, Luna, Minerva, Pax, SALUSM Triviam Venus, Vesta, Victoria. Goddesses of the Greeks include Eos, Heva, Selene, Athena, Gaia, Hecate, Fortuna, Hestia, Nike. The British goddesses are Andraste, Irish, goddesses are Macha, Morvvigan, and other nations directly or indirectly worship and sacrifice to this being as mother earth, great mother, good nature feminine life force or motherhood blessings.

This shows that goddesses are found and are worshipped in the cultural and religious traditions around the world. The existence of these two opposing beings Lucifer-god and Eve-goddess has created the natural and supernatural fight between them and that has resulted in numerous problems for human beings in the natural world. After Lucifer has defeated Adam and became the god of the Adam's world, he rather worked for the benefit of only the Caucasians as the

1- light bearer for Caucasians, but darkness for the Africans
2- guide to the soul that creates problems in human
3- provider of spiritual vitality for evolution
4- provider of intellectual independence and self awareness
5- provider of cognitive freedom to understand fake Jesus christ
6- spirit of independence cognition, wisdom in woven
7- opens the way for Christ (Steiner, 1954).

The fight between Lucifer-god and Eve-goddess is intense because Lucifer acts as god after he has defeated Adam, and claimed himself as the creator of angels and human beings, and the father of Jesus. In 2 Chro 26:16 Lucifer was replaced by king Uzziah who usurped the priest office. In Ex28, the writers replaced the name Lucifer with the title king of Tyre without a name, and explained the characters of Lucifer.

Lucifer hides under the title god and operates as a loving god to deceive humanity through the Old testament scriptures that he is a loving father. As soon as Lucifer succeeded in overthrowing Adam and became the god of this world Lucifer took the place of god, and Lucifer-god used his adversary personality called 'satan' to take the place of the hidden Lucifer as god's enemy.

The present cruel acts of god in the Bible show the luciferian totalitarian dictatorship judges that punish human beings and put them permanently on their knees to seek help from god, without a clear mind to ask questions why all these problems happen. The name Lucifer associates with Latin, but Lucifer appeared in Is14:20 and in the Hebrew manuscript, the name Lucifer was replaced with the Babylonia king and the personality force or spirit of Lucifer –Satan was absent.

It is important for human beings to know that the fall and the activities of Lucifer started in the first planet, the sun where lucifer god established his throne and made it the kingdom of god, and the scripture confirms Lucifer god as the prince of this world (John 14:30) and as the prince of the power of the air, as the disobedient being (Eph 2:2). This scripture describes the kingdom of Lucifer-god in the kingdom of the air, which is the solar system in the sky ruled by the power of the sun. The first level of the kingdom of heaven cut off from the upper parts of the kingdom of heaven starts from the sun sky down to earth.

It is within the isolated first level of the kingdom of heaven that we have all the planets. This shows that Lucifer had been in all previous planets before the planet earth. The type of beings who were created to restore the first level of the kingdom of heaven were unable to overcome the self-glorification of Lucifer, and those planets were one at a time closed down, until this planet earth was created. Adam and Eve were created to procreate angels to occupy the cut off first level of the kingdom of heaven that the beings in the previous planets could not because Lucifer, the fighter deceived them but he also deceived Adam and Eve and the whole world is on the wrong side, building the kingdom of god for Lucifer and human souls, instead of connecting with Jesus the revealed IAM, the Creator, to build the kingdom of heaven with the spirit of Jesus, for Jesus to connect the separated first level of the kingdom of heaven back to the heavenly realm.

This shows that the planet earth will soon be closed down, and another planet will be created, and another type of beings will be created, since human beings particularly the Africans have failed Jesus.

In the Roman astrology, Lucifer was the name given to the morning star, and that star is known by another Roman name Venus. This shows that the Romans have a link to the planet Venus.

Rodus from Germany sent his video around the world in which he confessed that 'white people are not really human. White people, originally from north Europe are from Arian group, that came from out of space from another galaxy, that came out to control the world of Blacks. We are from another planet who has their own language, wealth and do not want to share it with the black race'.

Whether you believe it or not, this is a very important information. This is an evidence that different types of beings were created by the IAM, through Jesus the IAM, but they were deceived by Lucifer and they failed to restore the cut off first level of the kingdom of heaven. The Venus was closed down, and when the kingdom was created for Adam and Eve, Lucifer continued deception and succeeded in allowing them to rebel against their creator, the IAM, and they lost the kingdom built for them by the IAM. In the planet earth, a very strong figure in the person of Eve, with her power given to her by Lucifer, she procreated human beings with Adam, when Lucifer was locked up for thousands of years. Adam died and Eve became the goddess and ruled the world for thousands or millions of years. When Lucifer was free, he first created what is called Noah's flood and killed almost all Africans, except the few that escaped with Noah (Mbosowo, 2010).

The scripture shows that Noah had three sons, Shem, Ham and Japheth (Gen7:13). The Bible does not name Noah's wife and the wives of the three sons. The truth is Noah was a prophet who preached against intermarriage for one hundred twenty years, and Noah did not marry. I just quoted a German who presented the white race as alien.

The name 'Shem' represents the alien race that came into the world that was built by the Africans, with the intention to mislead them to fail to restore the first level of the kingdom of heaven taken over by Lucifer by rebellion. They knew very well that the African race could have won the battle and when they came, they overpowered the African race, and distorted the truth for them to do the wrong thing and fail.

The above quotation from the German shows that the Luciferian race through Shem, that has extended from another planet to this earth, wants to make sure that the information that the IAM, the Creator created the first man Adam as the first African-god, and that African race owns this world, Luciferian race came from the already destroyed planet to control the Africans in this world.

In Is14';12, 2Pet1:19, the name Lucifer is replaced with bright morning star, all these are done to put the name Lucifer hidden under the title god and make him the almighty god, the creator of humanity, so that he can succeed in putting away the name of the creator the IAM, whom he rebelled against and was thrown out of the kingdom of heaven. This is the fight that Lucifer fought and continues to fight I AM for millions of years and has succeeded to keep the name IAM out and replaced him with the title god as the one who created the heaven and earth. The problem of humanity is not that we don't know the truth, rather it is that the truth is only known by the Caucasians who are directly from the Luciferian lineage, and that the truth is hidden from the Adamic-African race, the IAM created to restore the cut off section of the kingdom of heaven, but Lucifer the fighter, also Adam and Eve, the first family, just as he did to the created beings in each of the precious planets.

This rebellious behavior of deception has helped Lucifer to become god, and to establish to kingdom of god, which human beings in different organizations will praise and worship him as god to fulfill his desire to be worshipped, the envy and jealousy that led to his rebellion against the IAM, the creator. It is not the Caucasian who will solve the problems of humanity, rather it is the African race.

The reason is that Caucasian came from the already distorted planet though Lucifer, the leader, to deceive and enslave the Africans created to restore the first level of the kingdom of heaven that beings in the previous planets failed by Lucifer's deception. The Caucasians did exactly what Lucifer-god told them to do and they enslaved Africans for millions of years.

After millions of years of Africans beings enslaved by the Caucasian, Moses went into the bush and cried, suffered, prayed and asked why his people had been enslaved for millions of years and god did not answer their cry. The real creator revealed himself to Moses as IAM (EX. 3:14-15) and commanded him to tell his people to change from worshipping and calling upon god to calling upon IAM and instructed Moses that the change started at the same moment he has revealed himself to him. This shows that the Africans were calling upon the Lucifer-god who guided the Caucasian to enslave them. I believe that when Moses told his people, it became a laughing matter, as the enslaved Africans were acting in ignorance and were acting in ignorance and were afraid of their slave masters, and this deception and the slave mentality continues till this day.

Eve the devil: the presence of Eve, the goddess in the Old Testament and war between her and Lucifer-god

The Old Testament is a record of war between Lucifer-god and Eve-goddess, but the writers wrote it in such a way that human beings regard Lucifer-god as the almighty god and regard Eve-goddess as the devil.

It is importance to know first that the evil of god to humanity, particularly the African race started when Lucifer-god caused the flood 'Noah's flood' to kill almost all Africans on earth (Mbosowo, 2010). After the remnant with Noah had procreated and filled the earth and had been in different locations, Lucifer-god destroyed their center of development and scattered them (Gen11:4-9) and then helped the Caucasian racial group to destroy the existed Africans in order to control the earth. They succeeded after they has mixed with Africans and had stolen their culture, language, and power of progress. It was then that they created a name 'Yahweh' as their god, and the name Lucifer was hidden. All they did was known by Eve, the goddess, but writers hid it from Africans.

It was the Yahweh that became god of the Old Testament and developed the evil act against the entire African race. The war started when Eve the goddess, the first created African woman came to confront Lucifer god after they had succeeded in copying their documents from the ancient records of the Canaanites, the Egyptians and Mesopotamians and then labeled as evil whatever they left behind and then had authority to destroy them.

They had used this method to destroy Africans who owned the earth. The name 'Baal' in Hebrew means 'lord'. The scriptures in Judges 2:13; 3:7; 10:6, show that the Israelites were following the Canaanite god-Baal and their goddess Asherah, instead of their god Yahweh. This means that the invaders went into Canaan with the aim of studying the Canaanite gods and goddesses in order to turn things around for their own good and for the disadvantage of the Canaanites. They studied everything about Baal and developed the cult of Yahweh from the principles of Baal.

After they had established Yahweh as their god, they then defined Baal as the false pagan god who became the enemy of Israel.

Immediately the Israelites differentiated baal from Yahweh, they began to destroy the Canaanites for worshipping baal. In 2king18:4, the scripture shows how King Hezekiah destroyed the sites of baal worship and cut down the Asherah and broke into pieces the brazen serpent which Moses had made, just because it was the goddess with women.

The denomination of Baal-Asherah worship as evil before Yahweh was particularly because its principal adherents were women, and the center of worship was focused on a mother goddess. The war was built on the foundation of conflict between two religious groups as masculine against the feminine. It was opposition of men against women they defined as evil.

In Deut12:2, the scripture tells us that god ordered the destruction of those who worshipped the goddess in Canaan, and commanded the bloody massacres and demolition of status as places of worship and tear down their altars, pillars, carved images of gods. The leadership of women under the goddess was a threat to the Israelites and every effort was implied to destroy them. In the book of Num31:32-35, the scripture records the war by the Israelites in which they destroyed 'thirty-two thousand girls who had no intercourse with men'. In the 2kings23:4-15, king Josiah took the vessel, made goddess Asherah out of the temple in Jerusalem, and defiled the high place that Solomon built for goddess Ashtoreth, and broke into pieces the pillars and cut down the asherim and filled their places with the bones of men.

The attack on the worship of goddess was to put an end to the reing of goddess that gave women authority over the men. Prophet Jerimiah in his book, threatened the daughters of Egypts, Tyre, Sidon and Ascalon for worshipping the goddess and openly warned women for their intention to continue their worship of the queen of heaven and that they would meet with famine, violence and total destruction because of their insistence of believing in the goddess.

In Ezekiel chapter 8, the scripture shows the worship of the goddess under attack. As Ezekiel entered at the temple gate and broke through the wall, he saw all sorts of images, and snakes and repulsive animals and all idols on the wall, and he went further inside and saw people facing east to pray and to the north gate of the temple of Yahweh and saw women worshipping goddess Ashtoreh. In Ex. 9:4-7, Yahweh commanded the priests and other men to kill both old and young, both maids and little children and women and touch no men who had mark on their forehead.

In Iking18:19,40, the scripture shows that the four hundred prophets that Elijah killed were the worshippers of Baal and the goddess Asherah, who were with Jezebel who refused to worship Yahweh. That was an attempt to destroy the religion of the goddess through the incorporations of Judaism and Christianity.

CHAPTER SEVEN

Projection of Satan, The Spirit of Lucifer as The God of The Universe

The word Satan is the personified spirit of Lucifer. Satan means an adversary and an enemy. When Lucifer the archangel rebelled against the IAM, he was kicked out of the kingdom of heaven, and he lost his divine angelic nature, and his rebellious behavior become the spirit called Satan, meaning and adversary, an opponent. The word Satan explains the nature and behavior of Lucifer who rebelled against the IAM and after he was out of the kingdom of heaven, the new spirit in him was Satan, as the one who opposed the Creator and the rebellion was defined as witchcraft (1SAM15:23).

The explanations of the word Satan in this book refers to Lucifer'S spirit that he uses to run the spiritual organizations, as well as being an agent to rule over humanity, while he hid under the title god to hide his evil acts that came along with him when he rebelled against the Creator, the IAM. Satan is the main force and power that put the Luciferian principles into effect.

Satanic principles serve the supremacy of Lucifer who is acting as god in the place of Adam he deceived and overthrew. The scripture says that satan is the prince of this world (John14:30). This means that Lucifer is projecting his True mange of the adversary nature of the spirit called Satan, to control the world, while Lucifer himself is still in the body of the a beast, hiding under the title god to set up his principle and implement it. This force or power that makes up Satan, does all the operations, negatively for some and positively for some, All passages in the Bible with the word Satan represent Lucifer who is the god of this universe. The word Satan is the spiritual foundation of the secret societies, secret religions and occult groups that are legitimately owned and organiezed by the Caucasians racial group, withouth negative criticism, because Lucifer god is on their side, while he uses the devil force to steal, kill, and destroy (John10:10), all that the African racial groups are trying to do. While Lucifer is hiding under the title god, satan acts as his spirit and an agent to deal with human beings. For example the work of satan as the spirit of Lucifer, includes Job who was tested and tortured by satan, satan is the prince of the power of the air (Eph2:2), just to mention a few. All these activities show the work of Lucifer god through his projected spirit, satan. In Judaism, satan is defined as accuser or adversary. In Christianity, it is the serpent who tempted Eve to eat the forbidden fruit. In Islam, it is believed that satan was driven out of heaven by Allah for refusing to bow to Adam and his Creator. I want to make this clear that the Creator is the IAM, not god. After the IAM has created Adam as the god of the kingdom and of the land, he was given authority to rule over both the kingdom on the land and the sea, where Lucifer was. Lucifer was angry, and made all the plans to overthrow Adam, to become god, and he succeeded in overthrowing Adam with the help of Eve, and then became the god of Adam's world. This was the nature of Lucifer "to overthrow" the plan he started with the IAM, the Creator in heaven and failed.

Activities of Lucifer with his spirit satan as the god of the OT Bible

I have observed that most human beings in this world do not know that the concept satan is the spirit of Lucifer who was expelled from heaven because of his rebellion. When Lucifer rebelled, he was called satan, which means adversary, opponent, and enemy. The word satan was the personified nature of Lucifer that represented the spirit, power and a being that lives in Lucifer. Lucifer deceived Adam and became the god of this present world built by Adam. It is important to show the world that Lucifer is the god of the bible and he uses his spirit satan to run all the operations of this world. In this book, the IAM is presented as the Creator of the Kingdom of heaven and later created Adam as the god to restore the first level of the kingdom of heaven that was cut off by Lucifer's rebellion. It was Lucifer who deceived Adam and became the god of this fallen world built by Adam. This shows that IAM is not god and god is not IAM. Immediately after Adam sinned and disconnected from the IAM, Lucifer became the god of the world Adam built, and luciferian racial group took the lead while the Adamic racial group became the followers. The bible writers started their writing when Lucifer became god of this worl and they used lucifer's spirit satan to help luciferian racial group (Caucasian) to develop their own environment after Lucifer has reduced Eve, the goddess to deep on the kingdom of the sea and commanded her to attack and torment her own African race. The bible writers warned Africans not to follow satan because satan was evil and the reason was to prevent the Africans from self development, rationality and critical thinking that they received from Lucifer, the god who was their light bearer of intelligence so as to acquire power to be independent thinkers, to take care of themselves and acquire the craft-skill intelligence to develop their nations and that allowed Africans to remain as followers and obedient slaves. The present world is for the gods and goddesses using witchcraft system on the two major spiritual operations

1- Lucifer god satanic operations
2- Eve goddess devil operations

The two operations came into existence when Adam lost his divine lineage and became a slave to Lucifer, the deceiver. It was then that Lucifer used his rebellious spirit defined as witchcraft in a positive way to rule this universe for the benefit of those of his lineage, the Caucasian racial groups. The whole planet was ruled by the power of witchcraft until Jesus, the revealed IAM arrived and disrupted it, and restored the power of IAM through his name as the second Adam. After he had gone back to heaven, Lucifer Satan and Eve devil took back the fight and what Jesus did was distorted and corrupted because the Africans were too weak with slave mentality and could not keep what Jesus restored. It was the Luciferian lineage of Cain-Caucasian racial groups that took over and had ruled humanity till this day. The usurped ruling has put humanity in the physical and spiritual slavery, financial, marital, drug and alcohol problems, hatred lies, inequality, exploitation, oppression, imprisonment, jealousy, murder, theft, sexual sin etc. and these problems have prevented human mind from having a straight thought to ask questions about their unbearable problems. They lack the truth. Let us go into the bible and see the operations and the fight between the two opposing forces. In Eph 6:10-12, Paul pointed out that the whole universe is ruled by the prince of this world and his governmental powers, which are satanic, lucifer's spirit and his angelic beings. It was written in the bible because before Jesus came, Lucifer acted alone as god and he used his spirit Satan to rule humanity and human beings who did not know anything about the IAM and Jesus the IAM, regarded Lucifer, the god of this universe as the almighty god and worshipped him only until different racial religious emerged, and that resulted in conflict between and among the gods to see which god would be the leader.

The conflict between and among the gods resulted in the written of different holy books with a command to the followers to follow religion of their choice and not to go to another god. Religious laws and punishment were created and meted out to the breakers of those religious laws. These gods are reigning in different religions and cultural systems but Lucifer is still the prince of this world (John14:30), because human soul is his representative being in human, and he receives human souls after death for his kingdom. In Ezek 28:12-19, the scripture records the cover up information. In this passage the people who wrote the bible and knew that they could not get away from Lucifer with his rebellious nature, had to introduce the king of Tyre, in order to hide Lucifer who became god after he had deceived Adam with the help of Eve and Adam built this sinful world that Lucifer is god till this day. Lucifer has been the god of this world without any challenge until the Supreme Creator spoke to Moses with his real name IAM (Ex3:14-15) not god and later revealed himself in human form as Jesus, the IAM (John8:58). The reason the war between god and goddess and among the gods and goddesses has continued is that the truth about the Supreme Creator IAM and the revealed Jesus, the IAM has been suppressed in order to give Lucifer the godhead and allow religious gods to confuse people and keep human beings in darkness to fight themselves. In (Job2:6-12) the scripture recorded information about Job that had been misunderstood by people for thousands of years. The truth about Job's case is Job was holding unto his Creator, the Great IAM and as an ancient African with the truth, he did not worship Lucifer, the god of the bible, that represents the Caucasian racial group. Job determined to hold unto the IAM and because of that, he was persecuted and tortured by Satan the spirit of Lucifer, the god of the bible, who is the god of this world. Job had human soul, that is the representative of Lucifer Satan, the god of this world, but he did not listen to the dictates or commands of his soul.

In(2cor10:3-5), Paul is talking about wars with satanic powers as he puts confusion in human beings about god and how god gives Satan power to punish human beings. People do not know that it is Lucifer who uses his own spirit Satan to fight them. The soul in human being came through Adam and Eve into human race when Lucifer deceived them and that soul is the representative of Lucifer who is the god of this world. This then shows that Satan fighting human beings, is not really a fight, rather it is empowerment of human soul to function well for Lucifer- Satan -god.

In (2cor11:13-15),Paul presents how false apostles transformed themselves into angel of Christ, and how Satan transformed themselves into angel of light. Paul has provided explanations for visions or dreams that some people have about Jesus. Some people testify that they heard the voice of Jesus, but they only saw a light and not Jesus himself. This type off vision refers to Satan transforming himself into angel of light to deceive people with a voice to represent Jesus. Satan is Lucifer'spirit and it is working for Lucifer who is the god of this world (John8:44). I have a big question that will follow later. In 2cor2:20-22. 2cor10:3-4; Ipet5:8-9; Luke22:31-32. in ps34:7, the scripture shows that both Lucifer Satan and Jesus the IAM operate in this world for the benefit of humanity and Jesus gives his angels to protect those that are his from the evil acts of Satan. In 2cor2:10-11, Paul advised his hearers to forgive because unforgiveness is the character of satan, so that satan will not take advantage of them because of unforgiveness and that the satan's device is to make them not to forgive and then become his followers. In 2cor10:3-4, Paul shows that the followers of Jesus are fighting to pull down the strongholds of satan against them. Paul says that though one is following Jesus, the forces of darkness through satanic works are after the believer. In IPet5:8-9, Paul states that because of the presence of satanic activities, those who believe in Jesus are asked to be vigilant in order to avoid such evil powers. Paul's warning show the satanic control of the universe. My question is if the being that people regards as god in the bible is the same one that allows satan to cause all the sufferings to human beings, and even fighting Jesus, the scripture says is his son, whom he sacrificed to save people from sin, where is the effect of the death of his son Jesus Christ that he sacrificed? The time has come for people to take a second look at things and make a detail critical analysis of what they read and took it for granted. The bible scripture shows the war, conflict and evil acts between Lucifer-satan-god and Eve-goddess-devil, but Jesus came in as a Mediator, Redeemer and Savior to restore the original work of the IAM given to 'man' and' Adam' but was messed up by Lucifer during deception. The work of Jesus as the Mediator Redeemer and Savior will be discussed in a different chapter.

Luciferianism:

Lucifer defeated Adam and became the god of this world that Adam built. After people in the world have started to blame god for all the problems of humanity, Lucifer decided to come out of the covering of the title god and with his name Lucifer, he used his spirit satan to form his principles, ideology, philosophy and magical types of knowledge, through the concepts luciferianism, Satanism and other spiritual organizations for the Caucasian racial groups, as legitimate secret organizations for them. The following are the different types of satanic organizations. I want to emphasize that all religions in the world are not connected to the IAM (Ex3:14-15) and to Jesus, the IAM (John8:58). This means that all religious organizations are connected to Lucifer who rebelled against the IAM the creator and he was thrown out of heaven, in which he deceived Adam, and Eve became the god of this world, and this made Lucifer the founding father and god of all religions in the world today. Due to all the problems for humanity and the blame is on god, Lucifer refused the title god and decided to come out as Lucifer, the light bearer in order to present himself as a separate spiritual leader. This separation has made the title god redundant even the Jews write it as 'G-d' and gave different names like Yahweh, Jehovah, to the begins they worship instead of god. In each religion in the world, a name is given to who ever the people worship instead of the title god. It is then clear that Africans who followed the ancient religious system of the IAM that Moses gave to them were killed and another religion were given to those who were left behind as slaves and to make it worst, their languages were taken away from them to prevent them from seeking the truth. The languages of the colonial and slave masters allow Africans to think through their consciousness in which they have the spiritual advancement for technological breakthrough. This is my greatest concern because I had a dream." I was walking in the street in Egypt in the evening. Two people were going forward in front of me at about twenty yard apart. As I walked, I saw three African men sitting by the road side on my right. Immediately I was about to walk pass them, I heard them say in my language as: "Mme mbon ukanyin ibaha ke itie emi se nyin ikpino mmo nwed ekebene ebot ererimbot emi? Meaning 'are there no people from my place for us to give them the book that was used in building this world?. As I turned and said to them 'here I am'. I woke up because my wife shook me because my voice was out. This makes me to believe that Africans cannot move on because the divine mind they were created with was taken away by the Europeans who gave them their languages through colonization and slavery, and their spiritual understanding and the coverage to speak out were locked up.

The Projection of satan to identify
Lucifer as the spiritual leader

The church of satan:

This organization was founded on April 30, 1966 by Anton S. Lavey. The organization believes to be the first to open up and present the true nature of man as carnal beast that lives in a cosmos that is indifferent to our existence. Members believe they are those who do no embrace the concept of a soul imprisoned in a body, rather they represent pride, liberty and individualism, as qualities that those who worship eternal deities define as evil (ref3). The church of satanic brotherhood was founded in 1972, and practices true modern satanism and claims that members do not worship a devil, burn baby fat candles. In the modern church of satan, the development was founded to provide a church, an organization, a community and intellectual, collectively for the evolved members of the satanic religion within the modern world. Members claim to be the strength and the energy of the next generation, exploiting the potential of the cyber ago. The satanic international was started to spread the work of satan on the satanic international network for critical thinkers in order to put logic and reason above superstition and mysticism so that people will apply their will desire and talent to achieve their goals.

Synagogue of Satan:

The true name of Satan, the kabalist say is that of Yahweh reversed, for Satan is not a black god but the negation of god, They teach that the words Satan and devil do not represent a person, but a force, created for god, but which may serve for evil.The force is the instrument of liberty or free will and presided over the physical generation, under the pythologic and horned form of the god Pan (ref4). In Iking18:19, Jezebel's synagogue of satan is documented in which she has set up the table of satanic dinner in mount carmel, and she invited 450 prophets of Baal and 400 prophets of Asherta to eat with her in her place and the prophets had meal with the queen or goddess of witchcraft. That was the indirect way for Lucifer to build up his kingdom, this is the synagogue of Satan that Paul observed as it operated among the Corinthians (2cor11:12-14), that the people were false prophets with a pretence to follow Jesus, not knowing that satan masquerades himself as an angel of light, in Rev.2:20, the scripture presents Jezebel's synagogue of Satan in the church of Thyatira, as she operated as a prophetess and corrupted the people with the spirit of witchcraft. It was Jesus who pointed out:

'Nevertheless, I have a few things against you, because you allow that woman Jezebel, who calls herself a prophetess to teach and seduce my servants to commit sexual immorality and eat things sacrificed to idols' (Rev2:20).

Jezebel spirit of witchcraft is working in churches and religious organizations till this day, because the god at the head is Lucifer. Jezebel's spirit operates with fear and intimidation. Jezebel sent a message of fear to Elijah: may the gods deal with me, be it so severely, if by this time tomorrow, I do not make your life like that of one of them' (Ikig19:12). Elijah was intimidated and he ran away because of fear. He was afraid of the witch, and ran away instead of confronting her. He failed to finish the work that he was sent into the earth to do, and for that reason, he was taken alive to heaven and he reincarnated in the person of John (Matt11:14-15). He then completed his work of releasing the hidden information as recorded in the book of revelation that is the mystery to only be understood by the holy spirit revelation (Mbosowo, 2010).

Biblical synagogue of satan

It is important for Christians and others to know that the different types of satanic organization have their foundation in the bible. In the book of job, 'one day the angels came to present themselves before the Lord and satan also came with them (Job1:6). This scripture shows the alliance between Lucifer-satan and Lucifer as god. The book of Job shows the reality of how Lucifer-god employed his own spirit-satan to run the universe for him and deal with humanity, the way he wants. In Job2:1-7, Lucifer-god sent his spirit-satan to punish Job for his refusal to renounce his creator, the IAM. This undercover by Lucifer as god, has labeled him a weak god for all the problems and has promoted satan as a powerful being to be feared. It was then that Lucifer asked his people to establish organizations that present his authority openly. Such organizations as church of satan, wicca, freemasonry, Rosicrucian, Cross and holy grail, new agers, Illuminati, Gnosticism and Christians are found as members in all these religious organizations, and members in these organizations still use both the Bible and other materials and what they have done became a part of their lives and their practices became their daily habit. All these practices had given Lucifer-satan the upper hand as the ruler of the universe, and all the people in the world who promoted Lucifer as the light bearer, now fit into the satanic activities that rule the present planet earth, and they used satanic power to have technological development. In John5:9, the scripture says 'the whole world lies under the sway of the wicked one.'. If the entire civilization and development in the western world had been influenced by satan the spirit of Lucifer the god of this world, then the writers of the bible were hiding the truth in order to cover up the derogatory meaning of the word satan by the public. The Bible calls satan the god of this world 2Cor4-4) and he has succeed in keeping the cut off first level of the kingdom of heaven from reconnection, and will continue to succeed because human beings do not know the difference between the IAM, the Creator in the kingdom of heaven and god in the kingdom of god. When Jesus came from heaven, he said: 'my kingdom is not of this world (John 18:36) and that satan is the true ruler of this world (John12:31; 14:30; 16:11). The question is why should satan rule this world and god be silent? It is a very simple question and the answer will enlighten individuals. Satan is the spirit of Lucifer who is the god of this world and therefore god and satan are the same person, and god or satan cannot challenge each other. Both are one, Lucifer with spirit, satan. I want this world to know that this world is ruled by Lucifer the fallen angel who caused the separation of the first level of the kingdom of heave from the rest of the heavenly realm and during the restoration, Adam was created by the IAM and was given the title god but Lucifer deceived him and became the god of the this world that Adam and his generation built, and because of that disruption, this world became the kingdom of Lucifer-god. He owns this sinful world and when Jesus, the revealed IAM came, he said that 'my kingdom is not of this world'. let us stop all the religious propaganda and mind control in the name of god and face the truth that Lucifer satan controls this world by the power of witchcraft. the only person who fights him is Eve-goddess-devil.

Lucifer rules the world through different religious cultures and nations with different gods that represent him as the head of the universe. For example, there are many religions with different names for their gods, in cultural systems are the Egyptians gods Greeks gods, Chinese gods, Japanese gods, Middle east Canaan gods, African gods (Mbosowo, 2007). The war between Lucifer-satan-god and Eve-goddess-devil that had resulted in all the problems for humanity involved these two opposing groups of gods under Lucifer-satan-god and goddesses under Eve-goddess-devil. These wars that brought suffering and torments to humanity allowed Jesus, the revealed IAM to come down as the Mediator, Redeemer and Savior, as it is discussed in the next chapter. I want to close this chapter with what I have already said in order to present what you have not known. When Lucifer was locked into the body of the beast, he promised that every being that may he created, he would make sure that such being would be locked into a body like him. He deceived Adam and Eve and they lost the divine nature and spirit of the IAM their creator and Lucifer remade them with his spirit to dwell in the Adam's body that became sinful and carnal and that became the new Adam to procreate beings for him to form his kingdom on earth. He succeeded in making the beings for this world to live in the body of a beast. He uses his spirit satan to rule and control the world just like human beings uses their soul or spirit to do anything, but the soul or spirit is stocked in the body until after death. The only privilege is that humans speak. I want everyone to know this revelation. Lucifer still plans to seat at the throne of IAM in the third heaven till this day. He has set up his kingdom on earth through religious organizations and to prepare human beings with the soul in them as his representative to form the team that will invade the third heaven and dethrone the IAM, the creator and he will sit on that throne to fulfill his plan from the beginning. This is why many religious holy books, particularly the bible encourages their members to pray and turn their souls into Christ like. This is the process of building what people call the kingdom of god. This kingdom of god is Lucifer's preparation to go back to heaven for war with st Michael and his angels for the throne. Because Eve, the goddess knows what Lucifer did to her, to disconnect from the IAM her creator, has fought him for millions of years, already discussed in the previous chapters, and will continue to fight him. I want to present something that will shock most of you in the church. This is the world that Adam built after he lost the divine kingdom built for him by the IAM. When Lucifer deceived Adam and took over the world he created the three kingdoms as the kingdom of the air, his throne, the kingdom of the land where human beings live and the kingdom of the sea, where the one third of the angels who rebelled with him were locked into the body as sea creature live. This book discusses the three kingdoms of the sea, the land and the air, and that has set up the structure of the universe that we live in now.

This is the structure in which Lucifer the god of this world sets up to build his kingdom and the army to go back to heaven and fight the IAM to overthrow him and seat on the throne as the creator. He has not given up and he determines to succeed. As soon as his team is ready, this diagram will be fulfilled

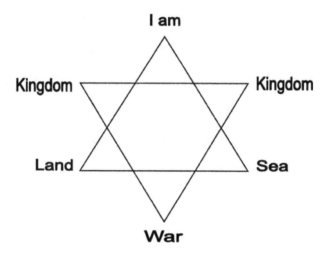

The war will take place and if he wins the two kingdoms will be merged for the human soul and the rebellious angels locked in the body of creatures will be free to occupy the throne and protect it for Lucifer as the creator. Those who are using this symbol are supporting Lucifer indirectly and they should know that whoever they call Christ is with Lucifer, the god of this world as his son and whatever people are doing in their religions has deceived human beings by turning the substance of gold into money as the god of the material world, and makes human mind to pay attention to material wealth and through that channel human beings lost the spiritual mind of reuniting with the kingdom of heaven as angels. The church and other religious groups have missed this truth.

CHAPTER EIGHT

The Revenge and Fight Between Lucifer-God and Eve-Goddess

Most people ask such question as: "why does God allow so much sufferings in the world." The entire humanity particularly the Africans, had been deceived about who God is, and people had been confused that there is a difference between Lucifer who deceived Adam and became the God of this world that Adam built, and the concept "world" that Adam built, and the concept of the word 'satan'. I have already discussed these concepts in the previous chapters, but I want to bring it here so as to present the work of satan as the spirit of Lucifer that works as god.

All the records of killings, murders, stealing, oppression and exploitation in the Old Testament by God, show the fight between Lucifer-satan-god and Eve-devil-goddess. Immediately Lucifer took over the world from Eve-goddess, he condemned Eve-goddess as the devil, and subjected her and the entire African race to the world of witchcraft, and covered them with the spiritual covering, so that they could/cannot develop their physical world. This means that all the development in the African continent is restricted to witch world.

Since Eve-goddess is the head and ruler of this world, this invisible world is then ruled by witches, and all the first-born sons and other men who are killed by witchcraft, are workers. All the sufferings recorded in the Bible against God is the lucifer's attempt to put human beings on their knees, particularly Africans, to follow him as God, and not to ask any questions, but to direct their attention and attack to Eve-goddess that he has labeled as the Devil and evil as their enemy. I want everyone to know that the human sufferings hang on the fight between the luciferian racial groups Caucasians and the Adamic race-African (Mbowoso, 2012).

This fight has been on till this day. Through racism, Lucifer-God has commanded the Caucasian racial groups to kill Africans who owned the world in different places around the globe, for his people, the Caucasians, to occupy, and such acts have offended Eve-goddess. How did they succeed in controlling the Adamic-African world.?

I want to say something so profound. Jesus says in Matt 12:29 'or again, how can anyone enter a strong man's house and carry off his possessions unless he first ties up the strong man, then he plunders his house'. Most people wrongly use this scripture in prayer to tie up the devil and take back what he stole from them. This is the real meaning of this scripture. The Luciferian racial groups mixed up with the Adamic African race all over the globe, and studied their culture, religious and source of power, and after they had known everything and rewrote all their found out as their own, they renamed the originals as evil culture, religion and language, and they then started to kill the Africans, in order to occupy the world built by Adam.

Here Adam, as the strong man of the house was bound when Lucifer tempted him and he lost his godhead to Lucifer and the luciferian racial groups Caucasians took over Adam's possession, and Adamic household generations suffered murder, genocide and loss of property, but Eve the goddess of the household reacted and took the position of authority, because of agreement she had with Lucifer during temptation, that she would be like god if she ate the forbidden fruit (Gen 3:5).

I know define racism as the evil by one's heart and the judgment by one's eyes toward another. Such ill heart feeling and quick eye judgment started in the spiritual, and has been practiced in the physical for millions of years till this day.

Through racism, the evil works of Lucifer who became the god of Adam's world are recorded in the Bible. For example, in Gen 7:23, the Noah's flood was the greatest natural disaster that Lucifer-satan-god used to destroy almost the entire Africans race, except Prophet Noah who escaped with a few Africans who listened to him and they were the remnants who reserved the African race (Mbosowo, 2010).

Gen 19:24 records the fake names for Sodom and Gomorrah, to cover up African heritage and thousand of lives were destroyed. The luciferian racial groups called Caucasians, used racism to judge the characteristics of Africans, based on their religious laws they made for Africans as their slaves (Mbosowo, 2015). It was through their religious laws that they judged African as sinner, inferior and non-human, who deserved to be killed.

Lucifer-satan-god commanded his people to kill Africans because they are different racial group with different culture, religion and to hide the original African names and places, they created different fake names for Africans they killed in different parts of the globe. All names in the Bible are fake. The Bible has recorded all Africans that Lucifer-satan-god killed.

In num 16:49, god killed 14, 700 Africans for complaining, Num 25:1-11 shows that 24,002 African were killed to stop them from mixing with the Israelites. In Judges 1:4, 10,000 Africans were killed with the fake names Perizzites, in Judges 7:22, God set up Africans against themselves and gave them swords and 120, 000 Africans were killed in the fight, in Judges 20:35-37, a holy war was fought and 65,100 Africans were killed; in 1sam 4:1-12, a lie was recorded that god killed 34,000 Israelites soldiers. The god of Israel fought Africans to take their lands, how did he turn against his own people in the war and killed 34,000 of his own? This is a lie and must be rejected; in 1 Sam 5:19, 50.070 Africans were killed because they looked into the ark of Israelite god, David was god's own man because he killed in different wars for god in 2 Sam 8-10, David killed 65,850 Africans in 2 sam8:13-14, I kings 11:15-16, I chro18:12, Ps 60:1, David killed 1403 in 2sam25:24, 1chron21:14, David has census that he was not asked to do and god killed 70000 Africans that he counted but he did not kill David. Ikinfs20:28-39, god killed 100,000 intermarried biracial mixed African, the grandparents of the people they called Syrians, in 1kin21:30, god made wall to fall and kill 27,000 Africans, the grandparents of the intermarried mixed Africans they gave the fake name as Syrians; in 2chron13:17-18, god killed 500,000 Africans who wanted to fight Israelites but the scripture lies that it was the Israelites, in 2chro 14:9-14, god killed 1 million African in Ethiopia, in 2chor 28:7 god killed 120,000 Africans who did not want to follow Lucifer-satan-god-Yahweh.

I have decided to present a few. There are so many records in the Bible showing the evil acts toward Africans who built the world as the original owners of this world built by Adam and his generations. The Luciferian Caucasian racial groups could not use their hands to do anything until technology was invented. As I said before, all the names for racial groups and places in the Bible are fake names that replaced the original owners of this world built by Adam and his generations. The Luciferian Caucasians racial groups could not use their hands to do anything until technology was invented. As I said before all the names for racial groups and places in the Bible are fake names that replaced the original names of the people and places. This was done mainly to deceive the Africans and hide the truth from them during the time of slavery till this day.

The entire world was built by the Africans, but because of the mistake that Adam and Eve made, by listening to Lucifer, the fallen angel and tempter and Lucifer became god of Adams world and that made Lucifer-god to kill millions of Africans in different places around the world for Caucasians, the Luciferian generations to occupy as it is seen today. The scripture says the Adam died at the age of 930 years but there is no record that Eve and Lucifer died. Eve the goddess who ruled this world for millions of years when Lucifer was in prison, became angry for what Lucifer-satan-god had done to her people Africans and she decided to fight back. The war between Eve-devil-goddess and Lucifer-satan-god is discussed in the next section of this chapter.

Revenge: the sources of natural disasters in the world today

The world has experienced different kinds of natural disasters, such as earthquakes, tornados, floods, tsunamis, wildfires, typhoons, droughts and famine as predicted by Jesus (Matt 24:3-7). The records of revenge by Eve-goddess to the killings of Africans by Lucifer-god, present natural disasters as war against Luciferian racial groups-'Caucasians'. Statistics have revealed the effect of natural disasters in different nations around the world. There are other areas, such as wars, ethnic cleansing, genocide, and religious persecution that make the earth a dangerous place for humanity. My aim is not to present the total records of lives, property and other values that had been destroyed by natural disasters, but to give a few examples, and then discussed the real cause of these problems, and provide proper solutions to it. It may be contrary to what people have suggested, but after they had applied their method, the problems are still increasing.

For example, earthquake, floods, tornados, landslides, wildfire etc. had destroyed lives property, cities and another values all around the world. Between 1887-1975, China lost almost 8 millions lives. Between 1881-2013 in Philippines, earthquakes killed 43,291 people. Between 1935-2016 Haiti lost almost six hundred thousands lives, the United States of America lost 64,890 lives to natural disasters between 1871-2017.

These are a few examples, but there are many other cases that happened and continue to happen in season by season in the air, land and the seas, particularly in the western world and I say that all these are happening as a pay back for what has happened to the Africans.

Professor Donald E. Mbosowo. Ph.D.

African natural disasters:

As a revenge, Lucifer-satan-god has done the following natural disasters to the continent of Africa. A research was done on natural disasters in the continent of African between 1974 and 2003 (CRED, 2003).

The findings show that 41% of the disasters in the continent occurred in the East African region in which the highest 128 cases of drought and the highest 162 flood cases, as well as 58 cases of disasters with economic damage, occurred in this region. In the East African countries like Kenya, Ethiopia and Sudan, the region experienced serious droughts in which as many as 11 millions people had been affected by drought in the entire horn of Africa. Food insecurity in Ethiopia has left almost 2.6 millions in need of emergency assistance. The serious drought occurred in the central part of Sudan, which affected at least almost a million people and half a million were at risk of famine. Sudan also experienced severed flooding in which 30 people died, 100 were injured and more than 25000 houses were destroyed.

During the same 30 year period, 24% of all the disaster occurred in the West African region, in which the worst 101 drought cases occurred, and with 98 flood cases, more than 100,000 houses in the capital of Ghana, Accra, were destroyed, Mali, Niger, and Senegal also suffered from drought, in which there was extensive economic loss, and Burkina Faso registered one of the heaviest rainfalls, in which over 40,000 people were to live in miserable conditions and 8412 houses were damaged. Also in the same period 14% of the natural disasters took place in Northern Africa, in which high number of 28% drought cases occurred, 74 flood cases and 26 disasters with economic damage were recorded. The finding also show that 11% of the total disasters occurred in the southern African, and 16% disaster of economic damage occurred here, and particularly in Mozambique, the cyclone flood killed 900 people, displaced approximately 4000 people in Maputo and destroyed the road network which linked the city with other provinces; while the central African region suffered only 10% of the natural disasters, in which 47 flood cases, 31 drought hazards and 8 cases of economic damages were recorded.

The researchers concluded that the problem of natural disasters in African is the result of climate change. They say that climate change increases weather and climate hazard and also increases the vulnerability of communities to natural hazards, particularly through eco-system degradation, reduction in water an food availability, and changes in livelihoods. People in many countries around the world also believe that the natural disasters are caused by climate change. Researchers and other professionals have assessed the natural disasters and made recommendations for the understanding of the physical and biological factors that contribute to disasters. A lot of technologies had been developed to monitor, predict and control the natural disasters, but it is increasing and many more lives and property are being destroyed.

Anyone can disagree with my perspective, but I perceived that all the natural disasters are caused by the result of the revenge and fight between Lucifer-satan-god and Eve-evil-goddess, in defense of African race and the Caucasian racial groups. Eve-goddess is fighting for the African race, because Adam sinned and died a mere man, even though Jesus came and restored him and religions confused people by giving the position to Lucifer, the fallen angel and rebel, and introduced fake 'Jesus' to deceive Africans. Lucifer-god is fighting for the Caucasian racial groups, in order to rule this world. All these natural disasters, including the problems of wars, violence, abortion, murder, diseases, and death are caused by the fight between these two opposing beings, and we must know the truth so as to be able to solve the problems.

Solutions to the problems

The war between Lucifer-satan-god and Eve-devil-goddess must be solved. I have already discussed in the previous chapters, the relationship between Lucifer, the tempter and Eve who was first deceived by Lucifer, in which later was labeled evil and was sent to the bottom of the deep kingdom of the sea. Apart from Eve-goddess fighting for African race, as the first created African woman, she as the mother goddess and goddesses world-wide, are reacting to the way Lucifer-god used men and religion to degrade and oppress women. Eve-goddess is angry with the African men who rejected their own creator and even Jesus when he came to save them and turned to Lucifer-god as their creator.

Eve-goddess is punishing African men for their spiritual blindness and the anger for the African men made her to take a decision in her counsel with the goddesses world-wide to fight men. Lucifer-god fights for Caucasians and maintain male status. The reactions of these fights resulted in different kinds of problems in the world as violence, murder, killings, tornados, flooding, wild-fire, wars, plane-crashes, seas storms and rains. The natural disasters come from the kingdom of the air, the kingdom of the land and kingdom of the sea. Theses three kingdoms are inhabited by beings in the natural and in the supernatural. Whatever we see as natural disasters are the results of the fight by these two opposing beings in the supernatural. The goddesses are angry, and the wars will not stop by using technology because it is a fight between Lucifer-god and Eve-goddess, and being supernatural fight, Lucifer uses his spirit satan to fight, while Eve uses her spirit devil to fight.

These fights had been on for millions of years and will not stop.

The only way to stop these problems is to overthrow both Lucifer-satan-god and Eve-devil-goddess and enthrone the Savior from the IAM (Ex 3:14-15) as the 'Mediator' 'Redeemer' and 'Savior'. His name is Jesus the IAM, who is the revealed IAM (John 8:58). He is not Jesus Christ, the son of god who is Lucifer-satan-god of this world. The scripture says that god sacrificed his son to take away the sin of the world (Rom2:35). Which sin? Is it the human 'sin-soul' that Adam and Eve received from Lucifer during deception and their religion condemned the goddess as the devil and women as evil beings? Or is it Adam's sin that was caused by Lucifer, who became the god of this world that Adam built, and human beings regard him as the almighty god? In a situation like this Eve the goddess would be very angry because Lucifer broke his promise to her that if she ate the forbidden fruit, she would be god but now he is the god is her position. Both of them have fought for millions of years and they will continue to fight till this planet is closed down, as it happened to the previous planets that the beings there refused to take the truth.

People talk about demons and blame demons for bringing evil to the world without asking themselves the question, who these demons are and where do they come from? It is important for religious people who believe that demons come from the devil so please listen to me. When Adam and eve sinned, the spirit of IAM the creator left them and Lucifer the deceiver remade them inn his own image and gave them his spirit that became the human soul. The human soul is the representative of Lucifer, the god of this world, and because Lucifer-god represents the male status, when men die, their ghosts join Lucifer as their god to fight the war with Eve-goddess, and when women die, their ghosts join Eve-goddess to fight Lucifer-god even if they are black or white. These ghosts are what Christians call demons who bring evil upon human beings. I want everyone to know that Lucifer-god represents the luciferian racial groups, particularly males, even though Eve-goddess represents the Adamic racial group African race, she also represents females in order to keep the women status.

Lucifer-satan-god fought and defeated Eve-goddess through religious organizations in which men identified the worship of goddess as evil and they destroyed all the worship places and held women in control. It was from then that wars started till this day. The present natural disasters are caused by spiritual fight and the technology will not solve these problems. Scientists talk about spraying particles into the atmosphere. I repeat this will not solve the problem.

The fight is not only with the natural disasters, but records show that more than 65 million men from 30 countries who fought in the world war 1, and there were over 35 millions civilian and soldier casualties, and over 15 millions died and 20 millions were wounded, also the casualties in the world war 2 totaled 70 millions people, over 40,000 homicides in 2017 worldwide, with El Salvador having the highest murder rate at 108.64 per 100,000. Civil wars fought around the world for economic gain, social and racial inequality, territorial gain, religion, nationalism, revenge, revolution against oppressive regime, internal ethnic cultural or tribal conflicts, had killed billions of people and had destroyed properties.

The only solution to these problems is to do away with the luciferian scriptures and messages that present the fight between him and Eve and enthrone Jesus, the IAM, the creator, and bring back the hidden truth, that was destroyed, and the lost scriptures and then write a new scripture for humanity to follow and know the true Jesus, the IAM, the savior and the great I AM the creator, 'not god'.

After the IAM the creator has seen all evil done to humanity by Lucifer-satan-god and he sent his word into the womb of a woman, Mary, and the 'word' became a being inside her womb and she delivered a being called Jesus (Luke 1:31). He sent that word to become a person, in order to come as a 'Mediator' between the two evil beings, and to redeem the suffering human beings, and became their 'Savior'. Jesus came as the revealed 'Word' of IAM (Jh8:58) to save the lost and correct the lies that were taught to human beings and put back the truth given to Adam at the beginning before he sinned by listening to Lucifer, the rebel and fallen angel.

When Jesus came and went through the suffering, persecutions, imprisonment, death and resurrection, he saw what would come upon human beings in the world, because the two evil beings, Lucifer-god and Eve-goddess will not repent and stop their evil fights. It was the duty of African men to take the leadership in presenting the message by Jesus to the world, but they were killed and those who were left alive, were enslaved to live in fear, and they were given the distorted and corrupted scriptures about what Jesus did, and Africans lived in confusion till this day. The Africans men then failed to represent Jesus, the revealed IAM, as the creator, rather they turned to represent Lucifer-god as their creator 'He' and that angered Eve-goddess who saw that African race is supporting her enemy. That was why Eve-Goddess rose up to fight in revenge, and all these natural disasters, wars, violence and destruction of human lives and property are the results of the fight between Lucifer-satan-god and Eve-devil-goddess, all these are happening to all human beings irrespective of race, color or religion. All these will stop when all the distortions in religion, history, language and science are corrected for the truth to come out and the corrupt distorters will repent with public apology.

The message of fake Jesus Christ must be destroyed and the truth about Jesus the IAM, the revealed IAM the creator must be preached and practiced, so that humanity will be connected to the creator of life, and love will prevail to bring peace and harmony to the world. It is not what Adam and Eve did that brought all sufferings to the world, because Jesus, the IAM came corrected and restored it with his life, rather it is Lucifer-satan-god who wants to keep the world to himself, so as to have praise and worship to himself, that he did not have in heaven, and that has caused conflict between him and Eve-goddess, who knew that the problem with Adam was solved by Jesus.

I want to advise everyone that this fights and wars will continue between these two beings, to see who will win and rule this world since human beings are blind to the truth. We should do away with religious lies, deception, confusion, exploitation and enslavement that were established by Lucifer-god, to support what he calls the kingdom of god. All these evil acts will not produce good result because religions are cultural, racial and oppressive, with the aim of producing the strongest race as the strongest group, with god or goddess as the overall head of the universe. The evil will continue and will soon become the order of the day that will turn human beings into monstrous beings. If we reject the true solution, very soon, the air will be polluted and airplanes will not be allowed to fly, the kingdom of the sea will not allow ships and other containers, while the kingdom of land will not allow human beings to be comfortable. The result will be to close down the planet earth, as it happened to the previous planets.

I had a dream, and in that dream, I was in a group of people with Caucasian and Africans. The discussion in the group that last almost all night till I woke up at 5am, was that human mind was filled with lies, and the mind must be cleaned up, so that people can receive the "truth." The question was, how will that happen if people have been used to their racial, religious, cultural and political belief systems? The answer was that people know the right thing to do, but they use lies, oppression, exploitation and enslavement for control. The truth that came with Adam was lost when Lucifer deceived him and he gave him his nature and spirit as human soul, that became agent of sin (Gal5:18-21; Rom7) and the people that Lucifer-god chose as his own, got the authority to write every information for the benefit of Lucifer who became the god of this world.

Jesus, the IAM from the creator, the great IAM came and restored the truth, but after he has gone back to heaven, Lucifer, the god of this world empowered religious leaders to present distorted and corrupted scriptures to people, and this had been believed for thousands of years till this day. We have to reject these religious systems and disconnect from the two beings, Lucifer-god and Eve-goddess who are fighting and connect with Jesus, the IAM, so as to receive the truth from the Holy Spirit (John 21:25).

There are a lot of misunderstandings by most people, particularly scientists. Most believe that the natural disasters are caused by the climate change and base their perspectives on technological and human functions or activities, but do not know about the two opposing spirit beings that are fighting. I read form NASA's Apollo and lunar reconnaissance Orbit missions news of May 16, 2019, that NASA has announced their mission to the moon, which is named 'Artemis' after the Greek goddess of hunting for the year 2028.

I have already discussed 'Artemis' as one of the strong goddesses. This then means that before NASA makes any journey to the moon, the mission must be attached to the goddess that owns and controls the moon. This is an induction that America must take permission from "Artemis' the goddess before they can go near the moon, the kingdom designed by Eve-goddess when she ruled the world for millions of years before Lucifer succeeded in becoming the god of this world and pushed Eve-goddess into the deep of the kingdom of the sea and set up his own kingdom with the 'sun' called 'day'. As long as Eve-goddess is alive, nobody can go into the kingdom of the 'moon' without permission. The good news is that NASA wants to have a woman as one of the astronauts who will set foot on the moon. They are wondering what words the woman astronaut will speak when she arrives there. This is my advise: prepare the woman astronaut as a goddess. She will be able to connect well with goddess in the kingdom of the moon.

NASA with their mission 'Artemis' plans to land on the south pool of the moon, but the astronauts won't touch down and settle, but will plant a flag, take some pictures and bring some rocks home. This plan is still technological, and will end in a failure, and will not solve these problems for humanity as it happened in the previous planets. The only way to explore the moon, is to know more about it as the kingdom of feminine power of goddess. People plan to go and make their homes in the moon. This is not possible. The mistake that the beings who inhabited each of the previous planets, that led to the close down of those planets, is being made in the planet earth, and it will soon be closed down. The plan by American astronauts to return human beings to the moon, may be an invasion of the kingdom of a goddess, and may not be possible. Has this been done in the previous planets? It is important to find out whether the technological process was done in the previous and why it failed. I also read that the LRO has imaged more than 3500 fault scarps on the moon since it began operation in 2009, and some of these images who landslides or boulders at the bottom of relatively bright patches on the slopes of faults scarps or nearby terrain. These characteristics show similar images on earth, meaning that the beings that inhabited that planet or kingdom did not do the right thing to make it permanent and connect it to the heavenly realm. What are human beings on earth going to do in the moon, instead of doing the right thing on earth and make it the last planet and connect it to the heavenly realm, the throne of the great IAM. The image of quakes in the moon are the results of Lucifer attack on Eve's kingdom of the moon.

The immediate solution to this problem is to disconnect from Lucifer-god and Eve-goddess and connect back to the IAM, the creator, through Jesus, the IAM. The connection with Jesus the IAM to solve the problem is discussed in chapter nine. This truth is very important because Eve-goddess is very angry and decides to fight to the end because Lucifer the fallen angel thrown out of heaven, deceived her and Adam, and became the god of this world that Adam and his generations built. Most people in the world turn to god and to goddess and use the name 'Jesus' as the middle savior, and the religious scape goat, not knowing that Jesus, the IAM, came as the revealed IAM, the creator, to restore what Lucifer destroyed. The main reason why the problems cannot be solved is that people are not using the real Jesus, the

IAM, an African, who was killed and sacrificed as the head of all the slaves, not knowing that he was the revealed IAM (John 8:58) and would rise to save the slaves. After his resurrection to confirm the truth that he taught, Bible writers distorted the information and excluded all his teachings from the scriptures (Mbosowo, 2015). The only way Jesus can help, is to restore the real image of Jesus, as an African. Eve, the goddess will finally win, and the world will be closed down.

CHAPTER NINE

JESUS, THE IAM as the Mediator, Redeemer, and Savior

FIG 5
I AM
Throne of I AM the Creator

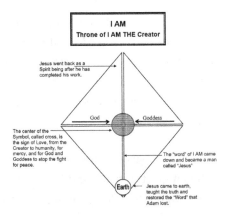

The truth that Jesus taught for a thousand or more years, are corruptively mixed with the records of the evil acts of the wars done between Lucifer-satan-god and Eve-devil-goddess in the Bible.

Physical Representation of the wars between god and goddess: David the warrior: The Beloved of God

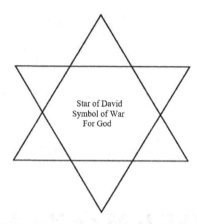

Star of David
Symbol of War
For God

The work that Jesus did was rejected and anything he did was distorted and corrupted before it was written in the Bible. A great fighter David, fought for god and killed millions of Africans, the owners of the world and took their lands, and then changed the original names of the people who owned the land and also changed the names of the lands (Deut 12:2-3).

The Holy Spirit revealed to me the meaning and purpose of all the wars written in the Bible that people interpret as satan fighting god and people turn to god for solution. David was chosen to fight and prepare the army for Lucifer –god to go back to fight the IAM and Jesus, and overthrow the IAM and sit on the throne, to be back in heaven where he was thrown out for rebellion. This is what the churches are doing because the people do not know the truth but rather the scripture says that everyone will appear at the judgment seat of Christ (Cor5:10).

This is for Christ not for Jesus, because when Jesus came, he did not judge anyone, rather he taught the truth and his truth created confusion among human beings who were lied to for too long, and that brought division between those who believe Jesus and those who disagreed with him, and that led to persecution, hatred, death and resurrection.

Jesus will not come back to judge anyone, rather he will come back to pick up those who yielded to his spirit, and had crucified the soul, the Bible calls flesh, and will carry them to the second heaven, and after turning the world upside down, to restore the lost kingdom built for Adam, he will then return his own down to occupy the kingdom and connect back to the second and third heavens, and the original structure of the kingdom of heaven with three levels will be restored (Mbosowo, 2015).

I don't want to go into the ancient origin of the star of David, rather I want to limit my work to the work of David in the Bible. David was a friend of God because of many conquests he made for the God of Israel, because the war for the original globe was also carried out among different racial groups under their different religions and their gods, and in the process, David became the warrior for the Israelites as the chosen people by Lucifer-god. He conquered Jebusites and renamed the place as Jerusalem (Ichron11:4-7). He conquered other places like Philistines (Isam18:24-27), the Amalekites (Isam30:1-31), he was anointed King of Judah (2sam2:1-11), the king of Israel (2Sam5:1-4) and as the king and the great warrior and the symbol of the star of David was given to David. This star of David is known in Hebrew as the Shield of David, and it is a recognized symbol of modern Jewish identity in Judaism and has also been used in Christian churches as a decorative symbol many centuries before its first known as used in a Jewish Synagogue. The symbol was used as a sign of power to make those who use it to stand strong against their opponents, with all their energy to win in order to retain the image and the spirit of David. In Is 49:2, Heb5:12, the scripture describes the word out of the mouth like the sharpened sword. This shows the power of the word. Since from the beginning Adam lost the 'Word' and everything became carnal and natural, human beings then used natural objects like guns, weapons and ammunitions to fight and kill one another in order to control and take possession.

This is not a major part of my discussion. I just brought this up in order to make a statement out of the symbol. In 2Cor 5:10, the scripture says that

Christ will come to judge. This refers to Christ the son of God, not Jesus, the revealed IAM. Jesus, the IAM will not come with the sword to fight as people try to interpret the scripture. The lost of the divine 'word' resulted in 'sword' from spiritual to physical and that empowered David to become the giant or warrior with the symbol as the 'star of David'. This violence was encouraged by Lucifer –god of this world, who wants to build this world as his kingdom, in opposition to Jesus who wants to bring peace, love, and harmony to humanity.

FIG 7: THE NATURAL WORLD

Fig 7: Natural World

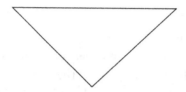

The first part of the star of David in figure 7 shows the natural world that Adam built and Lucifer took over. Lucifer was thrown out of heaven and he is down here to establish his kingdom as god, but because he is a fighter, the second part of the star of David, shows in figure 8. I am not trying to enthrone Lucifer, but he is a fighter who has fought and deceived all creations in all the planets, and unless we are wise he will try to win again.

FIG 8: Lucifer's plan to fight back

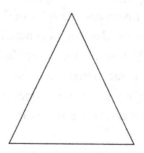

Lucifer's plan to go back to heaven to fight to overthrow the IAM after he has formed his kingdom of god on earth. In Figs 1 and 5, the lower part is the first level of the kingdom of heaven that was cut off because of Lucifer who rebelled against the IAM, the creator and it was separated from the upper level of the kingdom of heaven. It was there that Adam lost the restored kingdom and was thrown out to build his own world, he built the present world we live in now, but Lucifer deceived him and took over and became the god of this world, where he is building his army through human souls that their bodies are buried in the organized groups called cemeteries, where it will be easy to call them up to go up and fight. Lucifer is the god of this world and David was a warrior and he did a good job of killing human beings and god used him as the contact point to prepare his army to go back into the heaven to fight the IAM and take over the throne for himself as the creator.

It is important to know this revelation. When Lucifer deceived Adam and Adam lost the spirit of IAM and received another spirit from Lucifer, that is the human 'soul' the representative of Lucifer-god. When human beings die, the souls belong to Lucifer, the god of this world, and the bodies of the dead are organized well in a place called cemetery. When Lucifer-god is ready to go to war, he will go to the cemeteries and call those ghosts in groups to form the army for the war. This is what people who worship god do not know. Let me bring more explanations. In fig 1, the upper part is the third heaven where the IAM the creator dwell and Jesus came into the world as his 'Word' and went back after his work as the representative of IAM to save the lost. At the bottom of Fig1, is the first level of the kingdom of heaven cut off because of Lucifer's rebellion, where Lucifer dwells as god and Chist –Chistos, the Greek sun god was chosen as the son of god and Chist represents human souls that was given to Adam by Lucifer during deception. This is very clear, the difference between the kingdom of heaven with the IAM and Jesus and the kingdom of god with Lucifer-god with chist.

When humanity had so much problems, the creator, the great IAM sent a savior to restore the destroyed truth given to Adam. Jesus came down as the revealed IAM through the 'Word' into the womb of a woman 'Mary' and the 'word' became human to fit with the human beings, to restore what

Adam lost through Lucifer's deception. Lucifer, the god of this world was ready to fight Jesus, because as he was born as a man, he had the human soul in him, as the meaning of taking the sin of the world upon himself since human soul was given to Adam by Lucifer, when he deceived Adam and he lost his divine spirit from IAM his creator, and because of Lucifer's representative in Jesus, Lucifer-satan thought that he would defeat Jesus.

Jesus was rejected by his family, friends, the Jews, and others and he was lied abut, imprisoned deserted, denied, humiliated, tortured, hatred, killed, buried, and he rose from the death. Upon all these persecutions, Jesus did not yield to the demand of the 'soul' in him to react, to what people did to him, and he did not sin. Jesus defeated Lucifer-satan-god of this world, by not yielding to the human soul that Lucifer-satan-god put in man to make him his own. Jesus went through all the tortures and taught the truth and restored the 'word' that Adam lost and went back to heaven to connect humanity back the IAM the creator.

FIG 9: Work of Redemption

<u>Fig 9:</u>
<u>Work of Redemption:</u>

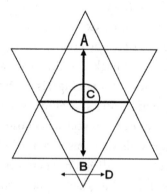

'A' is the throne of IAM, 'B' is the earth, 'C' is the cross marking the heart of love for humanity, 'D' is the fight connection between Lucifer-Satan-god and Eve-devil-goddess.

'B' is the earth where human beings dwell. After millions of years of fight between Lucifer –satan-god, and Eve-devil-goddess that resulted in human sufferings, Jesus, the IAM came down to earth as human and Redeemer. It took Jesus real love 'C' to go through rejection, hatred, persecution, imprisonment, death and resurrection, in order to save the lost humanity and through that love, he went back to heaven to connect humanity to IAM, the creator. It is important to understand the scripture. In Luke 1:28-31, the name that came directly from the mouth of the angel to Mary to be given to her son was Jesus. Any other name like chist was added by the Bible writers, with the intention to create something out if it. The word 'Chsit' is derived from the Greek word 'Chistos' meaning the 'anointed one'. This =was a title and a title cannot become his name, for example john went to medical school after graduation, a title was given him as Dr John, people can call him Dr. John, but the word doctor is not his name. The only scripture that Jesus presented himself as the direct 'word' from the creator is (Jh 8:58). Jesus said to them 'truly, truly, I say to you, before Abraham was, IAM.' this shows that Jesus is the 'word' from the creator IAM and the word became Jesus as the revealed IAM.

The word 'Chist' was formed from the Greek word 'Chsitos' meaning the anointed one, but the original word 'chistos' was the Greek god, worshipped as the 'sun-god'. In Luke 1:31, the scripture shows that the angel told Mary that the child to be born will be called Jesus. Jesus is the revealed IAM who came with power and authority and did not need any anointed from any earthly god. The Bible writer did the combination with fake anointing because they were ready to reject Jesus and either hid, corrupted or destroyed the truth that Jesus taught to the world, because of his race as an African (Mbosowo, 2015), so that the Greek sun-god will come out as his last name, and stand at the front to be used as the son of god of this world. This is why the word 'christ' was added to Jesus, and it is gone from one human language to another and religions have fought to retain the origin and source of the word 'christ' no matter what human beings are doing, the word 'chist' did not come out of the mouth of the angel Gabriel to Mary, and for that reason, it is not a part of Jesus's name and it must be deleted. This was done for the non-Africans to feel good that they are not under the spiritual leadership of the African race. Whenever the scripture, the preaching and lectures say that the birth and resurrection of 'christ' must be celebrated, they are refereeing to the Greek sun-god, 'chistos' as the son of god of this world, not Jesus the revealed IAM, who is the 'Mediator' 'redeemer' 'Savior' of humanity.

Jesus was the 'word' from IAM, made human in order to be able to communicate with human beings and Jesus as the revealed IAM should be called Jesus, the IAM and I have formed a name out of Jesus the IAM as I AM Jesus or AMIYESU, and any organization from Jesus the I AM, is Jesiamism or Yesiamism. This makes a direct transition, transformation and formation of a name that connects with Jesus, instead of bringing in a name of local deity called 'chistos-chist' from Greece to pollute the divinity of Jesus.

It is wrong for Jesus, the revealed IAM to be anointed by a local sun god. This was done for lucifer, the god of this world to regard him as his son. This is why Jesus warned his disciples in Matt 16:20, not to tell anyone that he was the chist. Jesus also declared that this world is not his, and it is not his kingdom. He was rejected denied, and persecuted, and after his resurrection, he went back to his throne in heaven, it was then that Greek sun-god 'chistos' was chosen and promoted to take the place of Jesus as the son of god, and the truth Jesus taught was either hidden or destroyed. This is why the work of Jesus does not have direct effect to change the world. Jesus the I AM sacrificed himself and shed his blood as the last sacrifice but the world continues to murder human beings to sacrifice to the god of this world because the real Jesus was hidden.

It then means that the use of the word 'christ' up to 555 times in Bible is the enthronement of 'chistos' the Greek sun-god. This is an indication that Christianity was formed from the Greek god of 'chistos' and it has no connection with Jesus, the IAM the creator. The diagram in Fig 10 shows that Jesus came as Mediator. Redeemer, Savior between god and goddess who are fighting and to disconnect humanity from these two forces and will connect those who will follow him back to the creator, the IAM.

Religion have confused people by covering up the real creator, the IAM and then introduced human beings to god who is Lucifer that was driven out of heaven because he rebelled and he became the angel of light, deception, and people follow him as their almighty god and Eve, the goddess is fighting him for his evil acts upon humanity till this day. This is the fight that Jesus came to separate as the Mediator, in order to save humanity. The world is divided into two sections. The first section is the African race, that is controlled by Eve, the goddess because Adam, the first created African man failed and after he has ruled for a million or more years, that the Bible does not record, he died as a mere man; section two is the Caucasian race, controlled by Lucifer who deceived Adam and became the god of this world. In the western world occupied by the Caucasians the men were able to create religions and in the process made Lucifer their god and maintained male status, and be able to break their women away from the world council of witchcraft that was practiced by all women in the world, and were then created 'hell' for their women when they die, because of how women used witchcraft to do evil to men. In Africa, Adam failed as a man, and Eve took over as the goddess and as a woman to establish female status. In the process, the women witches control the world of witchcraft and then control the men, since there are no men who can created religion in order to set up a place for women when they die.

It was Eve, the goddess who applied witchcraft she got from Lucifer during deception to control men and any man who joins the religion of witchcraft will appear in their meeting as a female because it is the kingdom for women.

The Caucasian men who created Orthodox Religions has set up a boundary in their sanctuaries that women do not cross into the inner circle. In the Pentecostal religious gatherings where women are running the show, is completely controlled by witchcraft. African men will be controlled by women forever, until they get up and created a religion and deal with the power of witchcraft, and then create hell for their women when they die. African race suffers double portions of punishment, one is from god that has destroyed Africans all over the world and has enslaved them through racism till this day, two is from the goddess that punishes men and makes them ineffective in the world. Let me talk about the savior of humanity. People talk about the second coming of Christ. This is different from Jesus, because the word 'chist' that came from the Greek sun-god has always been on this earth in Greece and has never gone anywhere. The scripture says that 'do not suppose that I have come to bring peace to the earth'. I did not come to bring peace, but a sword. For I have come to turn a man against his father, a daughter against her mother, a daughter in law against her mother in law, a man's enemies will be the members of his own household (Matt10:24-26). This scripture was said by Jesus not Chist. In this scripture, Jesus is explaining the truth that when he came into the world and taught the truth, and how the truth created division among family members and it shook religious laws made to enslave humanity as recorded in the Old Testament, and that let to all his sufferings and death. The truth he taught was like a sword that pierced human heart and turned people against one another in disagreement and division due to belief and unbelief among people and finally a plan that got rid of Jesus.

The information about the second coming of the son of man is a mixed message. It involved Jesus and christ as two different individuals in the coming (Matt 14:27-30). When Jesus came he said that 'my kingdom is not of this world, if my kingdom were of this world, then my servants would be fighting so that I would not be handed over to the Jews, but as it is, my kingdom is not of this world' (John18:36).

The world we live in now is a sinful system built by Adam after he had lost the kingdom built for him by the IAM the creator, by listening to his wife Eve and Lucifer during deception. Jesus will neither build his own kingdom in this natural world nor in the supernatural realm, because these two realms are in this universe controlled by Lucifer-god who is building his own groups with human in the natural and also uses human souls after death to build his kingdom, the kingdom of god in the supernatural and all these activities have no connection with Jesus in the kingdom of heaven.

The scripture in Matt 24-27-30 as refers to chist with particular attention to V28 that the anti chirst will be fought and destroyed and the vultures will eat their corpses. This means that the David's army will destroy the anti-christ that is seen as the cause of the problem. The question is 'who are the anti-christ' that will be destroyed? The scripture in I Cor15:22, answers the question that 'as in Adam all die, so also in Christ all will be alive'. This shows that the Adam's lineage that is the African race will be killed; meaning the generations of Adam must be destroyed. This indicated that when the army of Israelites killed African the work of Jesus who came to save them will come to an end on earth.

These scripture talks about christ the son the god of this world, who will come with the army to judge and destroy those who are not on the side of Lucifer-satan-god to build up the army for Lucifer to go back to fight to overthrow the IAM the creator, who threw him out of heaven when he rebelled. These scriptures have nothing to do with Jesus, the IAM in heaven. During Noah's time, Lucifer destroyed the generations of African race with flood but Noah and a few people who stood with him escaped. This is what Lucifer is planning to do. He will destroy non-Jew/Israelites, so that there will be no division in the formation of his kingdom on earth with his chosen people and then use their souls to form his army to go up and fight the IAM and take over the throne in heaven for himself.

I am just making this short discussion in order to make as statement. It is important to know that all the religious wars that had been on in the world for millions of years are the results of David-Jewish-Israelite's army trying to form the right army to fight for Lucifer, the god of this world, to get back into the third heaven where he was thrown out because of his rebellion. David represents the power of the Israelites who are with the Lucifer-god as his chosen people and the chosen must do their best to fight and get Lucifer back to regain his place in the third heaven.

David's army has no been able to form enough strength of the army to fight for Lucifer, the fallen angel to go back into the third heaven to overthrow the IAM the creator to compensate Lucifer for making the Jews/Israelites his chosen people, and the main reason is the formation of different religions and belief systems, and many groups broke away from Judaism, and David's army was not strong enough to go for a fight and the results are the present wars and the plan to destroy and annihilate the entire humanity. The formation of different religions with different gods and believe systems, disagreed with Judaism/Israelites and that resulted in fewer human souls after death and the strength of David's army was not strong enough, because the so called the 'kingdom of god' was not properly established, since there were/are so many gods trying to establish their kingdoms, with their plans different from that of the chosen racial group. The trick is, Lucifer, the god of this world has created the concept of heaven for human souls after death and that could have put all the souls after death in one place for the kingdom of god, but many people do not believe in god and do not believe in heaven, and this has shortened the number of souls needed to form David's army, and since they cannot have enough souls to fight billions of angels in their heaven, the people turn to destroy human beings who have not joined them in their religious beliefs and form one army for the war. The world needs Jesus, the Redeemer and Savior.

The only solution to the world problems is to find out the truth that Jesus established when he came down as the Mediator, Redeemer and Savior. Human beings cannot bring a change to the world because they are unable to get back what Jesus did because it was distorted, corrupted and deleted. The only way to received the missing 'word' of Jesus from the Holy Spirit, is to do away with the Old Testament dirty records of the fight between Lucifer –satan-god and Eve-devil-goddess, and then received the missing from the Holy Spirit see (Luke 21:25). Jesus, the revealed IAM who came down as the Mediator, Redeemer, Savior, presented the truth from creation and was not in agreement with the Old Testament scriptures with oppressive laws, fights, murder, enslavement, racism, inequality, wars, stealing and destructions, and his 'word' came out as a 'sword' that pierced the hearts of the oppressors and created division, differences in opinions among family members, neighbors, communities, nations, and finally Jesus was rejected, persecuted and killed and his teachings were rejected and 'christ' was brought in to relate to the fabricated information about Jesus in the Bible, and Christianity was created as a cover up. David was made the king of Israel, and he created a powerful army to deal with the enemies of Israel and to maintain the position as the chosen people by Lucifer-god. His plan was purely religious in which Judaism controlled many racial groups and created religious bondages and spiritual slavery to those people in order to remain submissive. When some racial groups had spiritual awareness and broke away and formed their individual religious belief, David's spiritual and belief system were reduced and his plan to go up to fight in the third heaven was suspended while waiting for the second coming 'christ' to come down from heaven to save Israelites from destruction.

The aim of David's plan is still alive. The creation of weapon, nuclear and ammunitions that will result in nuclear war, chemical war will be to destroy the weak, so that those left behind will be controlled to join in the belief of forming an army to go up and fight for Lucifer-god to overthrown the IAM in the third heaven and put the entire heavenly realm under the control of Lucifer the fallen angel who became the god of this world till this day.

I ask everyone to pay attention to this revelation. The following scriptures have made specific statement that needs people to understand. In Acts 10:42, it says that Jesus Christ will come back to judge the living and the dead. In 2COR5:10, it says that all will appear before the judgment seat of Christ to receive compensation either good or bad for what each did in the body while alive. In Gal 3:13; it says that Jesus came and died and redeemed us from the curse of the religious laws, that let to his death and after he has risen and went back to heaven, false prophets, particularly Judaisers, came in and changed all what Jesus did to set us free from religious bondage and restored religious laws in a different corrupted and confusing writings and their taking away the truth that Jesus taught and replaced it with a command to obey and practice the religious laws, has put human beings in spiritual slavery. What the distorters presented in the corrupted work of Jesus, came in under their Greek sun-god 'chirstos-christ', whom they have appointed as the judge for the non-Jews/Israelites, who failed to practice the religious laws. This spiritual blindness keeps people particularly Africans in spiritual slavery, When Jesus, the IAM comes back, he will be here to pick up those who had disconnected from the god of this world, his laws, and he will connect them back to the IAM, the creator. This is Jesus, not christ.

I need people to know what the judgment seat of christ means. It is the christ, the son of god of this world, that the Judaisers inserted to become the chief Judge, when he comes, this is what will happen.

The Earth or Universe under Heaven.

FIG 10

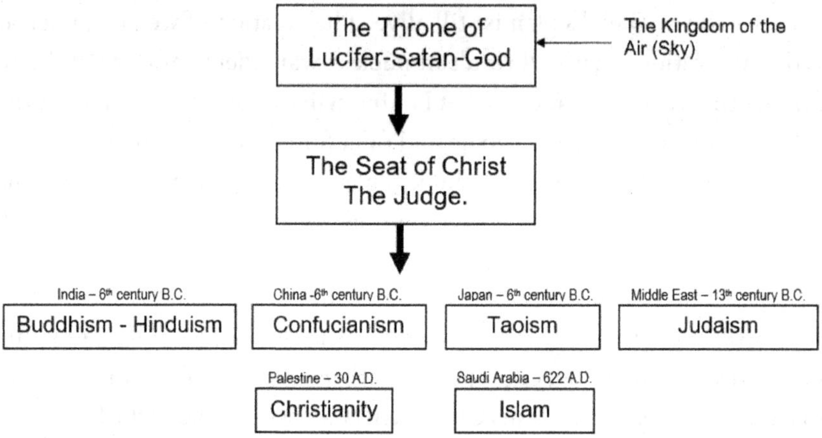

```
                    ┌─────────────────────┐        The Kingdom of the
                    │    The Throne of     │◄────   Air (Sky)
                    │  Lucifer-Satan-God   │
                    └─────────────────────┘
                               │
                               ▼
                    ┌─────────────────────┐
                    │   The Seat of Christ │
                    │     The Judge.       │
                    └─────────────────────┘
                               │
                               ▼
```

India – 6ᵗʰ century B.C.	China -6ᵗʰ century B.C.	Japan – 6ᵗʰ century B.C.	Middle East – 13ᵗʰ century B.C.
Buddhism - Hinduism	Confucianism	Taoism	Judaism

Palestine – 30 A.D.	Saudi Arabia – 622 A.D.
Christianity	Islam

All these religions are linked to different racial groups and they have their individual representatives, When we look at the judgment seat, it concerns only Judaism and Christianity where the Jews and Europeans enslaved African that do not have their religion and have no representative on the judgment seat, because they were deceived to rejected Jesus as their brother and Savior.

The coming judgment is only for the African race. The representatives from these religions will defend their people and those who do not have a representative will be killed. African does not have a religion and does not have a holy book to present, and all Africans will, not by flood as it happened in Noah's time (Mbosowo, 2010), but by the invented disease that will wipe them out of existence. Adam is the lineage of Ham-Canaan-African race, that was created to restore the first level of the kingdom of heaven that was messed up by Lucifer, the fallen angel, and Adam lost the opportunity through deception and luciferian lineage that took over, had tried to create the kingdom of god on earth for billions of years with failure. The only way for them to succeed is to destroy the entire African race. This judgment and punishment will take away all hindrances and will be left with those in the same plane and belief to form the David's army for Lucifer-god to go back to fight the IAM in heaven for the throne. This will be the end of the wars recorded in the Bible for people to fast and pray for themselves, not knowing that they are helping Lucifer-satan-god to recruit human 'souls' to form his 'kingdom of god' for the final war. This is the work of christ. Please do not include Jesus in this religious propaganda and illegal judgment.

I want to say this to the entire humanity. The preaching of the Gospel and the presentation of God and Jesus in the world are not the fault of the people who go into the profession, rather, it is the fault of those who wrote the scripture. It is either they knew the truth and refused to follow it, or they just followed cultural demand during copying and interpretation to cover the truth and sustain the activities of the local, racial and national gods, with the exclusion of the African race. The Gospel has been preached for thousands of years and the world is getting worst. This means that those in profession particularly Africans must put aside the old archaic scriptures and pray to received the hidden work of Jesus from the Holy Spirit read from John 21:25, which confirms that the Gospel is the selected scriptures to represent the culture of the writers with the exclusion of the enslaved. Immediately, this is done, the hidden 'word' of Jesus, the IAM will be revealed and the world will change from concentrating on the kingdom of god to facing the true revealed kingdom of Heaven. We are talking about the judgment, and it started with Judaism and Christianity. The question is 'why did the older religions not go into the judgment game? The older religions were under the goddess and they were dealing with their different god by worshipping nature. The process of spiritual evolution was based on the social status and good work, and it was individual responsibility to live an upright life for his soul to evolve higher after death, and some did not believe in heaven and hell. They did not use sword to make people accept their religious belief. The use of sword started with the modern religions of Judaism, Christianity and Islam, in which slavery, oppression, exploitation, inequality, wars murder, stealing and racism became the factors of controlling minorities, the weak and people with different skin color. The judgment of Christianity now will be through the christ, who will come down with the sword and judge the dead and the living and will destroy those who are not of their race, despite the fact that those outside their race have accepted their religion, but will be destroyed because of the color of their skin. For example, the great grand children of African descent who owned the world had been annihilated in Iraq, Syria, Turkey and others places in the West and Eastern world. In the continent of Africa, many Christians had been killed without notice, and all these had been done because of the color of skin and the work of christ. This shows that if the real Jesus, an African Savior was presented, Africans would not have been eliminated I other parts of the world.

The scripture in Heb 4:12 says: 'the word of God is quick and powerful and sharper than any two-edged sword, piercing even to the dividing asunder of soul and spirit, and of the joints and marrow and is a discerner of thoughts and intends of the heart.'

Most people do not understand this scripture because the original script might have been distorted by those who rewrote Paul's original script. The true definition of this scripture goes like this: the scripture is about those who accepted Jesus as their Savior. A person who accepts Jesus as his savior, has two beings living in him 'soul and spirit'. Any person who does not accept Jesus as savior, has only one being in hum 'soul'. Adam listened to Lucifer, the fallen angel and lost the divine spirit of IAM the creator and Lucifer the deceiver remade him in his own image and gave him his own spirit the human 'soul' that answer s to Lucifer the god of this world. When Jesus came as the reveal IAM (Jh8:58), he said that his kingdom is not of this world (John 18:36). The 'spirit' comes into the person who accepts Jesus as Savior, and both the soul that he was born with, for God and the 'spirit' for Jesus, live inside the person. Before Jesus came, every human being had only the 'soul' as the agent of sin that came into Adam from Lucifer, the fallen angel and the deceiver. After Jesus came and went back to heaven, he sent his spirit into those who accepted him as their Savior and that continues till this day.

The word as the two edged sword to divide 'spirit' and 'soul' that Jesus taught, that led to his death and he left and went to heaven, has been distorted and directed the corrupted version toward human soul that people pray to go to heaven after death, and the corrupted belief system had been presented that when one accepts Jesus, his soul will be transformed into the image of Christ. John 21:25 talks about the missing records of Jesus work on earth, that came to replace the evil works of Lucifer-satan-god and Eve-Devil-goddess upon humanity. When a person Jesus as his Savior and receives his spirit, he is supposed to have the revelation of the missing work-words of Jesus and when the words are received and preached, the words will present the difference and division between human soul and spirit and the truth will help one to crucify the soul and bring solution to humanity; and god will be angry, but the presenter of the truth may or may not be killed. Watch out, the preaching of the old records of laws, wars and fights between god and goddess will not change human heart and the problems of humanity will not be solved.

Since the truth is not preached, human beings do not know how to crucify their 'soul', the agent of 'sin' and the result is people pray for their souls to go to heaven, not knowing that their souls go to Lucifer-god to form his kingdom, the kingdom of god on earth and those souls are put together to form the army of David, to go up and fight to overthrow the IAM in the third heaven where Lucifer was thrown out when he rebelled against IAM. The David's plan was for Lucifer to take over the throne and rule the entire heavenly realm as a rebel and to compensate Lucifer for making the Jews-Israelites as his chosen people. Jesus came as the revealed IAM, to disconnect those who have accepted him as their savior from the god of this world and connect them back to their creator, the great IAM. Those who do not know this truth don't know how to deal with the two beings in them after they had accepted Jesus as their savior and this lack of truth has made it impossible for Jesus to have enough spirit beings for thousands or a million years to restore the lost first level of the kingdom of heaven.

Third level of Redemption: born again

Fig 11:
Third Level of Redemption: Born Again:

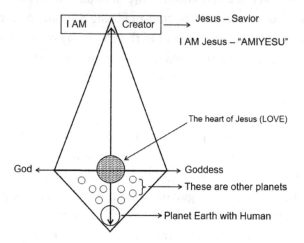

All the efforts by Lucifer, the rebel to turn the first level of the kingdom of heaven into his own kingdom, the kingdom of god took place in all the previous planets had failed. In the planet earth that human beings live now, he is using all measures, including religious mind control, wars and all kinds of oppressive acts to human beings to get them into his kingdom. In figure 11, the diagram shows the 'love' of Jesus as he came down from heaven to save the suffering humanity in the planet earth. His duty was to disconnect the human beings from the god and goddess of this world back to the IAM the creator, and to tell the Lucifer-satan-god and Eve-devil-goddess to stop fighting. His coming down from heaven to the earth and going back to heaven form the vertical dimension, his arms to the right and to the left to warn god and goddess from the horizontal dimension, and the formation of what we call 'cross' is the heart of Jesus, with four 'L' as the symbol of Love, that points to the four corners of the heavenly realms.

The change that Jesus brought down required the process of 'born again' by human beings. In John 3:5-7 (ESV)

'Jesus answered: truly, truly, I say to you, unless one is born of water and the spirit, he cannot enter into the kingdom of IAM (GOD). That which is born of flesh is flesh and that which is born of the spirit is spirit is spirit. Do not marvel that I said to you, you must be born again.'

Most people misunderstand and misinterpret this scripture. Many believe that when a person accepts Jesus as his savior, his soul will be born again and he will be like Christ. This is not what Jesus meant. The be born of water and the spirit refers to the two forces in the universes. Water: refers to the kingdom of the sea, ruled by Eve the goddess, while the spirit refers to the kingdom of the air ruled by Lucifer-god. When a person accepts Jesus as his savior, he must disconnect from the goddess kingdom of the sea through water baptism. This means that immediately he gets out of the body of water, he is totally disconnected from the control of the goddess, and immediately he received the Holy Spirit and speaks in tongues, he has disconnect from the control of the god of this world. If a person is born again and receives the Holy Spirit and still worship god and that person is born of the flesh and the Holy Spirit in that person will either remain 'dormant or depart', while his 'soul' the Bible calls flesh will be active as the representative of the Lucifer-god he worships. Born again demands a total disconnection from the god and goddess of this world and totally connect to the IAM, the creator through Jesus, the IAM. Any other process is the promotion of the worship of the god and goddess of this world and it is wrong to attach the name of Jesus to such corrupted belief system.

The religious game of serving Lucifer as god and Eve as goddess in this world must stop, the work of disconnection that Jesus is requiring from us involves disconnection:

1- from god to the IAM the Creator
2- from Jesus christ to Jesus the IAM
3- from human soul to the Holy Spirit

This truth of disconnection will intensify the war against those who will abide by the truth. The natural and physical wars that we see going on; are to eliminate the opposition racial groups that separate from the main

Davidian religious belief system and made their different religions and those who refused to follow them. The separation of theses groups had weakened the plan to form the kingdom of the god for the spiritual war. The wars will destroy those opposition groups and the remaining people will be controlled by fear and threat to believe in the Davidian religion and be willing to join in the building of he kingdom of god, Those that will build the kingdom of god, through the unified belief will be the ones to form the army by their souls after death in order to fight against the IAM, the creator. This is the knowledge hidden from people and the church. You can read the Bible and other religious books, but it is only the Holy Spirit who will reveal the truth to you from the letters that you read in those books, Jesus finished and went back to his throne in heaven with the hope that people will find the truth and disconnect from the god of this world so that he could come back to carry them up above this universes restore the lost kingdom and send his own back to occupy the restored first level of the kingdom of heaven and that will connect back to the rest of the kingdom of heaven and restore the original three levels of the kingdom of heaven.

Savior: Mediator to save:

In ITim2:6, the scripture records that Jesus: 'gave himself as a ransom for all…' he suffered and sacrificed himself to prove a true Mediator, with the desire to redeem and save all in the world. In Heb 2:9, we see that Jesus was made a little lower than the angel because of the suffering and death, since angels don't die, and for him to fulfill his work on earth, he has to become human. That was his willingness to redeem the whole world and humanity from the severe punishment given to human beings by the god and goddess. In Ijohn4:4:'And we have beheld and testify that the Father has sent the son as the savior of the world. The scripture was wrongly written. It should be, 'we beheld the proof that the IAM, the creator sent his 'word' that was lost and the word become human to save the world.

The creator sent his 'word' and his word became 'human' in order to communicate with humans and give them the 'word' as the truth to set them free from the religious bondage and spiritual slavery, created by the two opposing beings, Lucifer-satan-god and Eve-devil-goddess. In I John 4:15 (NKJV): 'whoever confesses that Jesus is the son of God, God abides in him and he in God.' Here again is wrongly written. The 'word' from IAM became Jesus, not the son of god, because god who claims to sacrifice his son to save humanity, is the one torturing human beings, and Jesus from the IAM, the creator is coming to redeem.

It says 'whoever confesses that Jesus is the son of god, god abides in him and he in god. Here means that, whoever confesses Jesus as the son of god, for god to abide in him, is linked to the Lucifer-god, in which Jesus, the IAM is trying to save. Jesus came and taught the truth. It is the 'word' 'truth' that he taught that must be in you and the true 'word' in you will communicate with Jesus, the IAM, and through the 'word', Lucifer-god and Eve-goddess will be defeated, and the kingdom of heaven will be formed, and the lost first level of the kingdom of heaven will be restored and be connected back to the rest of the heavenly realm.

In ICor15:49 (NIV): 'And just as we have borne the image of the earthly man, so shall we bear the image of the heavenly man.' This is a determination to turn things around for humanity. Adam was given the power for procreation by the 'word', but he lost it when Lucifer deceived him and he listened, and the divine procreation was then done through sexuality and spermatic deposit, and man was born carnal and earthly into a cage or body as prison, just like Lucifer in the body of a beast. Jesus as the revealed IAM the creator came and restored 'word', but after he has returned he heaven, those who objected to his teaching, either destroyed, corrupted it or hid it, and the result was/is human beings put the wrong and corrupted words in them to answer to Lucifer-god, that prepares the human 'soul' the agent of sin and representative of Lucifer-god, to form his kingdom, the kingdom of god on earth.

In Luke 2:10 (KJV), the angel said to the shepherd, 'behold I bring you good tiding of great joy, which shall be to all people.' Jesus came as a redeemer from the IAM, the creator to all the people, particularly the Africans, who were/are under the religious and spiritual slavery by the colonial masters. The word 'gentiles' or 'people' stands for a special group of human beings, known as 'African' and this information is different from the world in which the 'word' was corrupted with the letter 'L'= 'Lie' in order to merge African race with the Caucasians under colonial control and racial dominations. The good tidings delivered by the angels, had not been benefited by the billions of human beings because the true teachings of Jesus are not in the Bible, and the message was/is not directed to the right people (Mbosowo, 2015).

In Is49:6, the scripture shows that Jesus and message from Jesus directed to the enslaved Africans, were redirected to the Jews/Israelites, and they were given order to take the information to the African they enslaved for millions of years. They hid and kept to themselves the record of true teachings from Jesus and then created the evil religious laws to the Africans to believe, follow and no questions (Mbosowo, 2015). When Jesus has completed his teaching, he sacrificed himself as ransom in order to restore the lost glory of the IAM, the creator after resurrection (ITim2:6).

The work of Jesus as the revealed IAM John 8:58) to mediate, redeem and save humanity he created was changed to god and the mediation then was between god and men. This is wrong. Jesus came as the 'word' made flesh from IAM the creator, to mediate between Lucifer-god and Eve-goddess, who have fought one another for millions of years and human beings had been subjected to the effect of this flight till this day.

I want us to abandon religions and its practices that must have started in the first planet and were practiced through all the planets to the planet earth, but had not produced good result, because all theses religions involve lies, distorted and corrupted information relating to goddess and gods of this world. If we take Jesus as he is (Mbosowo, 2015), and present him for who he is as the mediator redeemer and savior, who has nothing to do with god, his truth and ransom self sacrifice will take effect and will restore the lost kingdom.

Paul states in Rom 5:10(KJV): "For if while we were enemies we were reconciled to god by the death of his son, much more now that we are reconciled shall we be saved by his life'. This is religious propaganda for god of this world, not the words from Paul who saw real Jesus.

The truth is through Adam, human beings became enemies to the IAM, and turned to Lucifer who deceived him and became the god of this world. It was the 'word' from I AM that became Jesus, who came in, taught the truth, suffered and sacrificed himself, and his death and resurrection were to reconcile us with the IAM, the creator. His suffering and death were to put an end to human sufferings and the shedding of blood. The real Jesus, his truth, suffering and death and resurrection, had been distorted, corrupted and destroyed (Mbosowo, 2015). The result is god of this world, who is fighting the goddess, is still killing human beings and cause all these disasters till this day. This means that Jesus is not the son of god, the Bible says was sacrificed to save humanity, rather Jesus is the IAM, revealed through the 'word' into the world, and the truth must be restored, in order to make the final sacrifice of Jesus's life effective and put an end to the killing and murder that is human sacrifice to the god of this world.

In IJohn3:2 (ESV): the scripture states: 'Beloved, we are god's children now and what we will be has not yet appeared, but we know that when he appears we shall be like him, because we shall see him as he is'.

This scripture means that through Adam's mistake we were disconnected from the IAM our creator and we were made the children of Lucifer who deceived Adam and became the god of this world, but the scripture says 'when he appears we shall be like him, because we shall see him as he is'.

A very intelligent child will ask you 'what are you talking about? Does it mean that the picture of Jesus that we see now is not the right one? This also means that if you are a child of god and you see that your father still kills, steals destroyed till this day, what else do you want to see. If you want to be a child of IAM and the name was hidden, and Jesus as the revealed IAM you are expected to see the real Jesus the IAM, and not only as the revealed IAM, but as an African, as he is. The scripture tells us that the real Jesus is hidden and on that day he will 'appear-appearance' presents image and image shows the feature and the color of the person, meaning when Jesus appears, he will be different from the white Jesus that has been presented to the world. this is the interpretation of the scripture in (IJohn3:2 (ESV)).

In Heb9:28, it says 'so Christ, having been offered once to bear the sins of many will appear a second time, not to deal with sin, but to save those who are eagerly waiting for him'.

It is important to be free from the religious bondage and spiritual slavery in order to understand the meaning of these scripture which were presented as a manual or code to cover up the truth that Jesus, the IAM, the creator brought to set humanity free from sufferings in the separate first level kingdom of heaven because of Lucifer's rebellion, that had been run by ucifer-god and Eve-goddess till this day. This is the meaning of the scripture in Heb 9:28. Adam sinned and lost the divine spirit of the IAM, his creator and received another spirit from Lucifer, the deceiver and spirit from Lucifer into Adam, became the human soul, and every human being is born with a soul. Jesus came as a redeemer and savior with the human 'soul' in him and he lived through suffering and persecution without yielding to the demand and temptation of the 'soul' that is the agent of 'sin' and Jesus finally killed the soul in him when he prayed in Mount Olives, before he went to the cross (Luke22:44). After his death and was buried Jesus went to hell and presented the death 'soul' to Lucifer, to show that He defeated Lucifer-satan and never owed him. When he was on earth, he taught on how to crucify the 'soul' but the Bible hid the truth and calls it 'flesh' and he also taught on how to disconnect from Lucifer, the god of this world, but religions misdirected human beings who follow Lucifer as their god, to pray for their souls to go to heaven. This scripture says that when Jesus comes back, he will not deal with those who have not crucified the 'soul' and disconnected from the god of this world, rather, he will deal with those who crucified their 'souls' and have disconnected from the god of this world.

People talk about the second coming of Jesus. This is different from the second coming of Christ as the judge to judge the dead and the living. Jesus is not coming back to do any further teaching, but to apply 'redemption' 'savior' and to rapture those who had disconnected from the god of this world, and were waiting for his arrival, because Jesus has completed his work of redemption and savior in his first visit. Majority of people accept as Lord and Savior, but are still the children of god, and they pray for their souls to go to the kingdom of god. All these godly activities on earth, have nothing to do with Jesus. This is why the love and compassion, shedding of blood and teachings of Jesus he left behind when he came are not effective, and the preaching of Jesus to the world for thousands has not brought any change in the world. Please accept the truth and be free from religious bondage and spiritual slavery. Lucifer-satan-god and Eve-devil-goddess are punishing human beings under religious lies and deception.

In Matt 24:29, Jesus said 'immediately after the tribulation of those days shall the sun be darkened and the moon shall not give her light, and the stars shall fall from heaven'. This means that after Jesus had returned back into this world, and picked up his own, the 'sun' created by Lucifer -satan-god will be eliminated and the light of the moon created by Eve-devil-goddess will be no more and the starts created by Lucifer-satan-god to guide the kingdom of the air, will be removed. When all these are done, the dark world will be turned upside the buried and the dislocated lost first level of the kingdom of heaven that was disrupted by Lucifer's rebellion, will be restored and his followers will be sent down to inhabit and the disrupted choir will resume and continue to worship the great IAM, the creator as angels. This is when the kingdom of heaven will be restored for the creator and his angels. Everything about god, goddess and human beings will disappear. Listen to this scripture in John 5:39-40:

Search the scriptures for in them ye think ye have eternal life, and they are they which testify of me; and ye will not come to me, that ye might have life (KJV)

The ancient prophets prophesized that in the midst of all the problems of murder, killings, stealing, exploitation, oppression and enslaving of humanity, there will come one who will give you life and Jesus revealed himself to them as the one with that life and pointed their resistance to come to him to have life. Those who knew that Jesus came to redeem and save the enslaved Africans, killed him and corrupted the truth he left behind and gave the distorted information to the slaves, who then believed it and turned their attention to the slaves masters as their helpers and worshipped their gods as the source of help. This is a warning to the world. All the lies must be corrected and the hidden truth about Jesus as an African must be restored quickly or this planet earth will be closed down as it happened to the previous planets that refused to 'repent'. The 'word' speaks, disconnect from the gods and goddesses of this world, and forget the ancient scriptures about them, and hold unto Jesus and have life.

CHAPTER TEN

Conclusion

I am not summarizing the book. I hereby present a few points. The problems in the world are caused by fights between Lucifer-satan-god and Eve-devil-goddess. Technological development will not solve the problems, and will go on for another millions of years until the planet earth is closed down as it happened to the previous planets. Lucifer was a created angel who sinned and was kicked out of heaven, and Eve also was a created being who sinned and was stripped off of the divine nature, and both of them became enemies of IAM, the supreme creator. Adam messed up and died a mere man, but there is no place in the bible or any other source, showing that Eve or Lucifer died. Adam was heavily punished by dissolving him back to the 'substance' from which he was created, and that was the end of the title "God" given to him by the I AM, the Creator. When the IAM sent his word to become 'human' called 'Jesus' to correct what Adam lost by his mistake, Lucifer, the fallen angel who became god in Adam's place, helped different racial groups to create religions that enslaved the African race that Jesus came to save, and those same religious groups turned against Jesus, hated, persecuted, imprisoned, oppressed, and finally killed him, and all his work had been distorted, corrupted and destroyed to confuse Africans, in order to keep them under religious bondage and spiritual slavery. Eve, the first created African woman was/is not happy to see how the entire African race had been reduced to the bottom of the universe for billions of years. This happened because the day Lucifer was released from his locked in prison (Rev20:7-9) in the scripture, I describe 'out of prison' as ability to speak, and it was that same time that Lucifer created religious organizations, and through religious manipulation and control, Lucifer locked African mind into the religious grave for millions of years till this day. This is why Africans cannot speak to change their situation. They are afraid of the slave masters and only believe what is given to them, instead of confronting those people who lied to them and kept them in the religious bondage and spiritual slavery. I have said this and I want to say it again. Rev 13 talks about the being called 'beast' and many may not understand it. Lucifer was locked into the body of a being called 'beast'. He walked around as human being but could not speak like other creatures, and in Rev 20:7-9, the scripture says he began to speak, he was/is walking around as a beast, and uses his spirit 'satan' to rule the rule, and he is the god of this world till this day. When people pray and curse satan, they are indirectly cursing their god, and the angels of their god will increase human suffering indefinitely. People believe without question, even if condition does not change. Afraid is the word. The Bible does not tell us how long Eve was with Lucifer after deception before she went back to Adam. The Bible states that Adam knew Eve and she gave birth to Cain, then another child Abel (Gen 4:1-2), but the same Bible in gen 5:4, the scripture says 'And Adam lived an hundred and thirty years and begat a son in his own likeness, after his image, and called his name SETH'. This shows that after Lucifer had deceived Eve, she was with him for 130 years and had Cain and Abel, meaning Cain and Abel were not Adam's children, but Lucifer children who introduced luciferian lineage into the natural world. this is an indication that Lucifer's time and sexual relationship with Eve had produced a group of beings before Eve went back to Adam, and the Bible does not report. It then means that after Eve had a sexual experience with Lucifer and had children for him to form a luciferian race, she went back to Adam and after she had convinced him, she invited Lucifer to transform him. Lucifer went and created sex organ 'penis' on Adam and Eve taught him how to have sex. It was after 130 years that Eve disconnected from Lucifer and Adam's sexual union with Eve, resulted in the male child called Seth.

I want to make some clarifications. All the beings-angels, created by 'man' and Adam who sinned by listening to Lucifer were all locked into the body of lower beings as animals and were not allowed to speak till this day. After Lucifer was released from prison and was allowed to speak, all the beings that came after him were locked into the body as prison, but were/are allowed to speak as humans, because after he has rebelled against the IAM, and was kicked out of heaven to remain under water from thousands of years, he was locked into the body of a lower being called 'beast'. The enslavement of Adamic generation by the Luciferian generation has created problem between Eve-goddess and Lucifer-god. The problems in the whole world will continue until African race disconnects from Lucifer- god and connects back to Jesus, the IAM, and accept him as their savior as an African who came to save them from religious bondage and spiritual slavery. Lucifer and Eve are fighting to see who will rule, since humanity was disconnected from the IAM, the creator.

A strong note:

Lucifer promised Eve that she would be like god if she yielded to his idea, and Eve agreed, she helped him to introduce his lineage into humanity, and then made Adam, the god of the kingdom to fall, after Eve had ruled this world for millions of years and Lucifer overthrew her and became the god of this world that Adam built, the fight started because Lucifer broke the promise he made with Eve. The problems in this world will continue, and finally the planet earth will be closed down. The only solution to these problems is to disconnect from both Lucifer-satan-god and Eve-devil-goddess, and connect to the IAM, the Creator through Jesus the I AM, as an African savior. Let us do away with the title god that was given to Adam and Lucifer took it after the fall of Adam, and we should also forget about all the religious names of deities created by Lucifer through religious organization, when he became god. I want the whole world to pay attention to this explanation.

Adam was made of a substance and that substance became a living being when the IAM put his 'Spirit-Man' inside the living being called Adam (Gen2:7). This means that when he listened to Eve and then to Lucifer, and sinned, the 'spirit-man' in him left and the divine nature of the great IAM left him and the Adam died, and his title god died with him. It was Lucifer who remade him in his image and gave him his spirit that has became the human soul that every human being is born with. When Lucifer took over and became the god, the new Adam and the new Eve under Lucifer procreated humans with soul that represents him as god. That was the beginning of the kingdom of god, which is different from the kingdom of heaven where the IAM and Jesus, the IAM dwell, that is the heaven where Lucifer, the archangel rebelled against the IAM and he was kicked out of heaven.

All religions base their judgment day on one's duties in life, good or bad deeds, by following the religious laws, and with different names and places for the deceased that we judge, but Lucifer, the overall god, will be responsible for all the souls judged and will use them for the purpose of forming his kingdom and prepare to fight the IAM the creator. Different religions may judge human souls to prove their religious laws, but Lucifer, the god of this world will use human 'souls-ghosts' for the war with the IAM in the third heaven as retaliation to fight back and get back to overthrow the IAM, the creator who threw him out of heaven. It is important to know that Lucifer who builds human souls to fight the IAM in the third heaven, must go through the seven previous planets in order to break through the seven previous planets in order to break through the columns, temples and spiritual systems that might have been formed with the beings that inhabited each of those planets, in order to get to the border of heaven to fight the angels, and the human 'souls-ghosts' must be the regenerated beings. People spend time to pray for their souls to go to heaven, not knowing that the human soul is an agent of sin that came from Lucifer, and will never connect with Jesus in heaven. The earth is in the first level of the heavenly realm that was cut of because of lucifer's rebellion. The reason there are beings on earth called humans is the failure of the beings in the previous planets to overcome Lucifer's lies, and follow the truth brought by Jesus, the revealed IAM, the creator. People mention Jesus name without connecting with Jesus, because Jesus connects with the IAM as the revealed Jesus, the IAM not with god and the Son of God. I want to remind people that the word 'marriage' was introduced by Lucifer after he has messed up Adam and Eve and then put the two together as husband and wife through sexual union. In this case, it will be 'soul to soul' as soul-tie to form one for Lucifer-god. The truth is Adam and Eve were two partners for the creation of special beings as the angels for the kingdom built for them by the IAM, and the two were given power to use the 'word' for creation and not sexual spermatic union. All that we see in the world, in religious organizations are for the human souls and their master Lucifer-god. We have only one heaven, the throne of the great IAM, where Lucifer was throne out because of his rebellion. Any other type of heaven taught in religious organizations, is in this world, where Lucifer-god has established his kingdom and as a rebel, he cannot send 'soul' to heaven. For anyone to get back to heaven, one must first accept Jesus, the IAM, as his/her savior, and receive the lost spirit of IAM and connect with Jesus, second one must disconnect from God and the fake Jesus, and then crucify his/her soul that is agent of sin. Since there is no marriage in heaven, the spirit of Jesus in the woman must go back into the man to become one as 'Elohim'. It is important to know that the spirit joins with the spirit and go to Jesus, the IAM in heaven, while soul joins with soul and go to Lucifer-god in the kingdom in this universe. The women who do not go back into the men to became 'whole 'will be sent to 'hell', a place god himself describes as a place of fire, with torment of pain and suffering reserved for the souls that rebelled against his commands. This shows that if you connect with Jesus, the IAM for heaven with the IAM, the creator, god has no power to touch your spirit, but will take your soul that belongs to him, in which you crucified as the dead being, because you did not answer to his commands, but you will connect your spirit with Jesus. The truth is, the earth and the previous seven planets are all located in this universe, and have no connection with the kingdom of heaven. Brothers and sisters, let us get the truth and disconnect from these fighters who started this fight from the first planet, and fought till today in the planet earth. They will not stop. We must leave them. Another important point is, if humanity wants to make progress and have peace on earth, all religious holy books with old history of oppression, slavery, theft, violence, wars, genocide, human sacrifice, murder, land theft and lies, must be abandoned, so that we can do away with the evil acts of gods and goddess who think that they have power and cause all these human sufferings when they are angry. This is the only way Lucifer-god can keep human soul that he gave to Adam and Eve during deception active, and subject humanity under Lucifer-god as the ultimate oppressor. If human beings are sensible, they will do away with all religions and its holy books, and receive from the Holy Spirit, the full word of truth that Jesus the IAM established, in order to help humanity. All religious organizations are doing business, and will not change. This business of following the word of god, after knowing the truth, is going backward with the old outdated stories, and no advancement in the spirit to bring love and peace into the world. It is unwise to cling to the distorted, corrupted and false information that keeps people on the dark concept of faith. That most have waited and died without receiving what they expected, not knowing that it is all about seeing the savior, but what does faith mean? F=false A=appearance I=introduced T=to H=humanity. False appearance introduced to humanity=FAITH, and that has blinded human beings when the real Jesus was hidden and fake European Jesus was introduces to the world called a 'Jew-Joshua'. This is like working with a dead plant. No wonder the power of Jesus resurrection cannot change the world for good, after thousand of years of preaching. It is now a challenge for people to wake up, disconnect from the dead past and receive the truth, to create the vision for the future (John21:25). It is sad that Jesus, the mediator, redeemer and savior does not have people to build his kingdom, because those who call his name and receive his spirit, still connect themselves to god, instead of the IAM, the creator, and because they are connected to god, they are working with their souls for Lucifer-god, not the spirit for Jesus. People take advantage of Jesus, the savior for his love, but respect god who punishes, tortures and kills, because of fear. There is a saying 'most people do not respect a kind and peaceful person, but rather fear and respect a tyrant and bully wicked person. This means that crying, praying, and fating all night and day to please god who oppresses you is a waste a life. Let us disconnect and have peace and harmony in the world. This is an advice to all men. Don't be blind to the truth, and be deceived by the material wealth. The human sufferings and pains in the natural realm show that Lucifer-Satan-God's hell for men is the material world, because the divine "WORD" that was spiritual was polluted with the "L-Labor" to become the WOR-L-D", AS NATURAL WITH MATERIAL WEALTH. It is high time we recognize Lucifer, the fallen angel as the official God of this world after Adam had sinned, built this world, died and lost the title God, and also recognize Eve who sinned and lost her divine nature, as the official Goddess of the kingdom of the sea, so that we can see clearly the fight and have the clear spiritual awareness to welcome Jesus, the I AM as the Mediator, Redeemer and Savior, for the manifestation of peace, love and harmony for humanity. Let us do away with the political, cultural and racial religions that have oppressed, killed, murdered and tortured human beings for millions of years. This is enough for the wise.

REFERENCES

Albright, W (1924) From the Stone of Christianity, Baltimore: John Hopkins Press.

Bamberger, Bernard J (2006) Fallen Angels: Soldiers, Satan's realm, Jewish Pub Soc. Of America, pp 148-149.

CNN, R.L. Stoneking, M, Wilsong, A.C. (1987) "Mitochondria DNA and Human Evolution" Nature vol 325:31-36.

Carr, William Guy (1997), Pawns in the Game, Dauphin pub Canada.

Center for Research on the Epidemiology (CRED, 2003)Thirty years of natural disaster 1975-2003, University of Catholique de Lourain, Press Universitaires de Lourain, Bruxelles.

Ford, Michael W. (2010) the Bible of the Adversary Succubus Pub., Spring Texas.

Gimbutas, Marija (1989), the Language if the Goddess, San Francisco, Harper and Row.

Graves, Robert (1948), the White Goddess, New York, A.A. Knopt.

Jones, Marie and John Savino (2007), Supervolcano: the Catastrophic Event that changed the Course of Human History, New Jersey: New Page Books.

Karlsen, Carol F. (1989), the Devil in the Shape of a Woman: Witchcraft in Colonial New England, Vintage Books: A division of Random House, Inc., New York

Kenyon, Kathleen (1960) Archeology in the Holy Land, Tonbridge, Ernest Benn.

Klein, Violet (1946), the Femine Character, London: Routledge and Kegan Paul.

Mbosowo, Donald E. (2007), Understanding the Bible and Creation, E. Book Time, LLC, Montgomery, AL.

Mbosowo, Donald E. (2012), Understanding Human Races: the Restoration of the Lost African Race and the Final Solution to the Problems of Humanity, Indiana: Xlibris Pub. Corporation.

Mbosowo, Donald E. (2010), Understanding the Book of Revelation: the Final Mystery of the Book of Revelation is finally revealed, Xulos Press.

Mbosowo, Donald E. (2015), Jesus, the IAM, the Savior whose image was hidden, now revealed, Indiana: Xlibris Corporation.

Muchmore, Elaine A; Sandra, Diaz, and Adjit Vork (1998) Structural Differences between the Cell Surfaces of Human and Great Apes'. AJ Physical Anthropology, 107 (2): 187-198, October.

Murray, Margaret (1921), the Witch Cult in Western Europe, Oxford, Cladendon Press.

Roberts, R.E. (1924), the Theology of Tertullian, London.

Robinson, D. (2010) the Emergence of Humans: an Exploration of the Evolutionary Timeline, New York: Wiley.

Steiner, R. (1954). The Dead Christ, the Opposing Powers of Lucifer, Ahriman, Mephistophels, Asuras (North Vancouver); British Columbia: Steiner Book Center, p18.

Stone, Merlin (1976), When God was a Woman, New York: Barns and Noble Books.

Summers, Rev Montague (1971), Malleuz Maleficarum of Heinrich Kramer and James Sprenger, Dover Pub, Inc, New York.

Webster's New World Dictionary, 1992.

Wolpoff, M.H. Hawks, J. Caspari, R. Hawks (May 2000); 'Multireginal, not Multiple Origins' Am. J. Physical Anthropology, Vol 112:129-136.

1- www.insidermonkey.com/blog/categori/list
2- https://en.wikipedia.org/wiki/moon
3- http://churchofsatan.com
4- http://sinagogueofsatan.org

Printed in the United States
By Bookmasters